"Wherever you are on your special-ne... your heart. It will give you inspiration as you finish the course God has for your precious family."

—LYNDA T. YOUNG, author of *Hope for Families of Children on the Autistic Spectrum* and *Hope for Families of Children with Cancer*

"Parenting a child with special needs is no easy task. I know: I've been there. I recall the day my daughter was born and our lives flipped upside down. I remember the financial uncertainties, the multiple hospitalizations, and the never-ending medical appointments and therapy sessions. But I also remember experiencing God's faithfulness in the midst. And that's where one's focus must rest in order to thrive amidst the challenges. This devotional will lead you to that place. Its words inspire hope in God and trust in his ways and wisdom. Let them lead you to the Father's heart, renew your perspective, and refresh your spirit."

—GRACE FOX, author of *Moving from Fear to Freedom*

"Parents of children with special needs too often inhabit a dry and thirsty land of isolation and despair. Kimberly Drew and Jocelyn Green's devotional offers living water and food for the soul to families wandering in the desert. Filled with stories and advice from parents who have walked the same road, and replete with promises and encouragement from Scripture, *Refresh* is an oasis of hope for families living with the realities of special-needs parenting. I highly recommend it."

—JOLENE PHILO, national speaker and author of *A Different Dream for My Child* and *Different Dream Parenting*

"'I had to pull over on the way home to cry. I had lost the mother-daughter relationship and future I had dreamed about.' When I read these words in the first pages of *Refresh*, I knew immediately that these authors trod the same path I had. They know the weaknesses of my heart and that God is the source of strength that sustains me. This devotional touches the heart and soul of parents with children who need special care, no matter how extensive that care may be. *Refresh* is truly refreshment along this trail given to us by God."

—SUSAN K. STEWART, author of *Preschool: At What Cost?*,

www.practicalinspirations.com

"Parents of special-needs children feel so alone and misunderstood, but Jocelyn and Kimberly give them a voice and a loving shoulder to lean on just when they wonder if they're going to make it. With empathy and encouraging words from the Lord, coupled with stories that will tug at every parent's heart, *Refresh* is more than a devotional—it's a lifeline of hope."

—JANET THOMPSON, founder of Woman to Woman Mentoring, speaker, and author of *Forsaken God?*

REFRESH

Spiritual Nourishment *for* Parents *of* Children *with* Special Needs

KIMBERLY M. DREW & JOCELYN GREEN

Kregel
Publications

Refresh: Spiritual Nourishment for Parents of Children with Special Needs
© 2016 by Kimberly M. Drew & Jocelyn Green

Published by Kregel Publications, a division of Kregel, Inc., 2450 Oak Industrial Dr. NE, Grand Rapids, MI 49505.

Published in association with the literary agency of Credo Communications, LLC, Grand Rapids, Michigan, www.credocommunications.net.

The authors and publisher are not engaged in rendering medical or psychological services, and this book is not intended as a guide to diagnose or treat medical or psychological problems. If medical, psychological, or other expert assistance is required, the reader should seek the services of a health-care provider or certified counselor.

Any undocumented stories and quotes from individuals in this book are from private interviews conducted by the authors. In each case, the persons and events portrayed have been used with permission. To protect the privacy of these individuals, some of the names and identifying details have been changed.

All Scripture quotations, unless otherwise indicated, are from the Holy Bible, New International Version®, NIV®. Copyright © 1973, 1978, 1984, 2011 by Biblica, Inc.™ Used by permission of Zondervan. All rights reserved worldwide. www.zondervan.com

Scripture quotations marked ESV are from The Holy Bible, English Standard Version® (ESV®), copyright © 2001 by Crossway, a publishing ministry of Good News Publishers. Used by permission. All rights reserved.

Scripture quotations marked NASB are from the New American Standard Bible®. Copyright © 1960, 1962, 1963, 1968, 1971, 1972, 1973, 1975, 1977, 1995 by The Lockman Foundation. Used by permission. www.Lockman.org

Scripture quotations marked NKJV are from the New King James Version®. Copyright © 1982 by Thomas Nelson. Used by permission. All rights reserved.

ISBN 978-0-8254-4403-6

Printed in the United States of America
16 17 18 19 20 21 22 23 24 25 / 5 4 3 2 1

> I will refresh the weary and satisfy the faint.
>
> JEREMIAH 31:25

CONTENTS

— Eight —

Branching Out: Touching Others' Lives Through the Journey

ACKNOWLEDGMENTS

From Kimberly:

I would like to thank the Lord first and foremost for saving me and for the hope and joy he gives.

I'd like to thank our families, specifically my parents, Ron and Kathy Adams, and my in-laws, Jim and Jerrine Drew, for loving Ryan and me through the difficulties of raising a child with special needs, and for supporting us in more ways than we could ever count or repay.

Thank you to my grandmother, Evelyn, who paved the way for how to raise a child with disabilities in the 1950s. Your story has given me strength to do what was necessary more often than you realize.

Abbey, you've opened my eyes in more ways than I could ever capture in a book like this. Thank you for being you!

Jayden, you are such a joy to me. Your heart for sharing your faith makes me want to do the same.

Cooper, your hugs and laughter make even the darkest day seem OK and help me to stay thankful.

Elizabeth, you are changing me already and I love you with all my heart.

I thank my husband, Ryan, for being my best friend and biggest fan even when I don't deserve it. I love you for every ugly and beautiful moment you have walked me through in this journey of raising Abbey. There isn't anyone else who could be a better daddy to her.

I would like to thank our prayer team, and my sharks, for praying us through this.

Thanks to my sister Kyleigh and friend Alli for being my biggest cheerleaders in life and encouraging me to write.

A heartfelt thanks to all the parents who shared their stories. I am inspired by you, truly.

I want to thank Jocelyn for believing that this devotional was worth writing and for helping me through the entire process from start to finish. You are such a dear friend to me, and it was my honor to do this with you.

I can't forget our agent, Tim Beals, who believed in this book and in us! Your work on our behalf is appreciated more than you will ever know.

Finally, I would like to thank the team at Kregel who made this book come to life. Fourteen years ago I was a new mom to a child with special needs, and I needed this book. I pray that through your efforts, many will be encouraged in their walk with Christ, and that others would come to know him because of it.

FROM JOCELYN:

As I reflect on all the families who have touched this book project, whether by praying for it, contributing to it, recommending parents for us to interview, or inspiring us, I am overwhelmed with gratitude. Special thanks to our prayer team for interceding on behalf of this book and to all the parents who shared their stories with us so that they might encourage others. In addition to the bloggers and authors we quoted, the following parents carved out time from their busy schedules to do personal interviews specifically for *Refresh*: Rebekah Benimoff, Penny Clark, Leslie Jurado, Courtney Morrison, Tonya Nash, Carly Nicodemus, Amanda Paragon, Allie Powell, Priscilla Rhoades, Alana Sankey, Allison Shelley, Laura and Craig Slezak, Kathryn Sneed, Laurie Wallin, Gloria Williams, and Rob and Anne-Marie Wurzel.

Thanks, as ever, to my husband, Rob, for his undying support even in the midst of grad school and working full time. Thank you to my children, Elsa and Ethan, for sharing me with my book babies.

I owe thanks to my parents, Peter and Pixie Falck, for making sweet memories with Elsa and Ethan while I've been on deadline.

Thank you, Kimberly, my precious friend, for reaching out years ago with the idea for this book. Every moment devoted to this project with you has been an honor and a privilege.

I echo Kimberly's thanks to our agent, Tim Beals of Credo Communications, and to the team at Kregel Publications, for bringing this book to readers hungry for refreshment.

Above all, thank you, Lord, that your light is brighter than any darkness. Thank you for being our very hope.

INTRODUCTION

D ear Friends,
There are many books out there on how to raise special children.
This one is about raising up the parents.

Some of you are just joining us with a new diagnosis. We know how scary and overwhelming that time can be. Some of you are starting to find your way and are learning how to navigate the medical world and school system. Some of you are veterans and have been loving and serving your child with special needs for a very long time. But we all have something in common: our children. They were fearfully and wonderfully made in the image of God (Gen. 1:27; Ps. 139:13–16). They are changing our lives, and the lives of those around us, every day.

Just as you pour yourselves into your children, we want to pour hope and courage back into you. We want to refresh your spirit by speaking biblical truth directly to the unique aspects of your particular lifestyle. As you read this book, you'll meet dozens of other parents on a journey similar to yours, whose children represent a wide variety of physical and mental challenges. Know this, dear friend: you are not alone. Regardless of which particular diagnoses are mentioned in *Refresh*, the struggles and joys borne out of them are ones you can relate to. We want you to meet the parents who share their stories here, but most importantly, we want you to meet Jesus within the pages of this book. The message of hope is the thread that binds these stories all together.

That message is the person and work of Jesus Christ. We hope and pray you know him personally already. If you don't, or if you're unsure, please refer to "Knowing Jesus Personally" in the back of the book. For those who already have a relationship with Christ, we pray that this book will be a great encouragement to you in your walk with him. Whether your faith is dormant or flourishing today, know that we've been praying for you for years. God longs to meet with you, no matter where you are on the journey.

As you read through these devotions, ask God to be with you and to open your heart to his Word and his Holy Spirit. After each devotional there is a prayer you can pray and a series of questions. Take the time to really think about how you would respond. We encourage you to journal your thoughts. If God is working in your heart or teaching you something new about himself, share it with your spouse or a close friend.

We echo the heart of Paul in his letter to the Colossian church: "My goal is that they may be encouraged in heart and united in love, so that they may have the full riches of complete understanding, in order that they may know the mystery of God, namely, Christ, in whom are hidden all the treasures of wisdom and knowledge" (Col. 2:2–3).

God is always at work. These pages are a testament to the work he is doing in the lives of everyone who participated in any part of this devotional. From all of us to all of you: feel loved, be encouraged, pursue Christ, press on.

With sincere love and gratitude,
Kimberly M. Drew and Jocelyn Green

ONE

Uprooted
When Life's Landscape Changes

I pray that out of his glorious riches he may strengthen you
with power through his Spirit in your inner being, so that
Christ may dwell in your hearts through faith. And I pray
that you, being rooted and established in love, may have
power, together with all the Lord's holy people, to grasp
how wide and long and high and deep is the love of Christ.

EPHESIANS 3:16–18

LIFE IS SHORT, ETERNITY IS LONG

Kimberly

Therefore we do not lose heart. Though outwardly we are
wasting away, yet inwardly we are being renewed day by
day. For our light and momentary troubles are achieving for
us an eternal glory that far outweighs them all. So we fix
our eyes not on what is seen, but on what is unseen, since
what is seen is temporary, but what is unseen is eternal.

2 CORINTHIANS 4:16-18

When Abbey was very little, we moved out of state and started the
search for a whole new medical team to treat her developmental
delays. At the new pediatrician's office, the doctor looked her over and
worked with her muscles. When the words "cerebral palsy" came out of
his mouth, I stood there with my own gaping wide open. I had to ask
him to repeat himself. In a casual second to him, my world went from
"delay" (with the hope of someday catching up) to a lifelong diagnosis
of disability. I had to pull over on the way home to cry.

I had lost the mother-daughter relationship and future I had
dreamed about since the day they told me, "It's a girl." Predictions of
the future, paired with memories of my own childhood as a little girl,
flooded my heart with grief. As the extent of our daughter's disabilities

unfolded, I realized I would never hear the sound of a little girl humming and singing through the house. I would never watch her skip or play teatime with her dolls. All the moments that I longed for in this life would never happen the way I had hoped.

At some point in the grief process, I realized I had put my hope in the wrong future, and that's why it hurt so badly. It was why I could not heal and move on. The Lord began to whisper eternity over my soul with verses like 2 Corinthians 4:16–18. To accept Christ is to accept the gospel; to live in Christ is to live in the light of it. Because of what Christ has done for us on the cross, we hold on to the treasured promise that heaven makes all things right. Heaven restores things to the way they were meant to be. There are no diagnoses or disabilities in heaven.

Revelation 21:3–4 says about this new heaven,

> I heard a loud voice from the throne saying, "Look! God's dwelling place is now among the people, and he will dwell with them. They will be his people, and God himself will be with them and be their God. 'He will wipe every tear from their eyes. There will be no more death' or mourning or crying or pain, for the old order of things has passed away."

Psalm 119:49–50 exclaims, "Remember your word to your servant, in which you have made me hope. This is my comfort in my affliction, that your promise gives me life" (ESV). God's Word gives us hope. This is our comfort, and the promises contained in his Word give us life.

Years ago, my mom started speaking the phrase "Life is short, eternity is long" over me. When this refrain becomes part of our souls, it helps transfer our affections and gaze from this life on earth to eternity with Christ. James 4:14 reminds us, "Why, you do not even know what will happen tomorrow. What is your life? You are a mist that appears for a little while and then vanishes." This moment we are in right now is not the end of the story. An eternal perspective gives great hope.

Father, help me to fix my eyes on you and not on my child's diagnosis. Help me to trust you not only for this life but for eternity. Restore to me the joy of my salvation, and with it the great hope of heaven. In Jesus's name, amen.

DIGGING DEEPER

1. How have you handled your child's diagnosis?
2. What hope and comfort do you find in the promises of heaven with Christ?
3. What can you do to foster this truth in your life?

MORE THAN WE CAN HANDLE

Jocelyn

My soul is weary with sorrow;
strengthen me according to your word.

PSALM 119:28

When Nichole was born with Down syndrome, the doctor told Ellen and Andy Stumbo that he was sorry. "Don't say you are sorry," Ellen chastised him. "Our baby is exactly who she is meant to be. God does not make mistakes."

"You religious people handle things better," the doctor replied.[1]

As a pastor's wife, Ellen told herself she ought to handle it just fine. But Ellen didn't want her baby. She was afraid of an unknown future full of limitations, and she mourned the loss of the baby she had expected to welcome. "And I was afraid that my family in Mexico would believe the very thoughts I wrestled with that were prevalent in our culture. That I had done something wrong and was getting what I deserved. Or that Nichole would never be whole. Although I knew it was not true, those lies would suck at my heart, like leeches, and I painfully would pull them out."[2]

It would be easier if she died, Ellen thought. *The pain and sadness I have is engulfing me, Lord! I don't know how I will ever be able to enjoy life again! I don't want this child!*

Her wish for her baby to die terrified her. Sadness, worry, and anger plagued her so intensely that it was a relief to Andy when he left home for work. Finally one night, Ellen asked him, "The Bible says that God does not give us more than we can handle, right?"

He paused. "[First Corinthians 10:13] is often taken out of context. That verse refers to temptation. God will not give us more *temptation* than we can handle."

"Well, does God give us more than we can handle when it comes to . . . life?" Ellen asked.

"Yes, honey. If we could handle it, we would not need God. But when we are given more than we can handle, it is then, and only then, that we realize how much we need him."

This is more than I can handle, Lord, Ellen prayed that night. *I need you to step in.*[3]

If you too feel overwhelmed right now, whether from a diagnosis, or a new test result, or the daily challenges that make up your new normal, then telling yourself you should be able to handle it will not help you. Jesus never said we should manage on our own. He said, "In this world you will have trouble. But take heart! I have overcome the world" (John 16:33). We don't have to be strong enough to conquer it all—Jesus is! And it is his strength, not ours, that we are urged to rely upon throughout the Scriptures:

The LORD is my strength and my shield; my heart trusts in Him, and I am helped. (Ps. 28:7 NASB)

God is our refuge and strength, an ever-present help in trouble. (Ps. 46:1)

I can do all this through him who gives me strength. (Phil. 4:13)

The next time you find yourself saying, "I can't do this," add two words on the end: "without you." You were never meant to live your life without God's strength, his patience, his grace. Your life may be more than you can handle alone, but nothing is too difficult for God.

Lord, this is more than I can handle on my own. Fill me with your strength. Grant me your love for my child. Thank you that you don't make mistakes—help me truly believe it! In Jesus's name, amen.

DIGGING DEEPER

1. What feels like more than you can handle right now?
2. What is one area you're trying to control but can't?
3. Identify a time when God's strength really carried you through.

OUT OF THE PIT

Jocelyn

He lifted me out of the slimy pit, out of the mud and mire;
he set my feet on a rock and gave me a firm place to stand.

PSALM 40:2

Ellen Stumbo's hands shook as she hung up the phone. The liver condition detected in her baby, the doctor had called to say, could be fatal. *"Oh dear Lord. I asked you to take my baby away, and now you are letting me have my way. My baby is going to die."*[4]

Guilt and fear knocked Ellen to the floor and unleashed a torrent of sobs. "I faced the dark hole I had been living in since Nichole's birth," she wrote on her blog. "It was deep, murky, and tight. It had become a prison. Life happened around me, yet I was stuck. My tears had been so abundant I would soon be covered in my own grief. And it was my despair over what I saw as unfair that would cause me to drown—not my baby, and not her diagnosis. The unending tears blinded me."[5]

Who among us has not spent time in a similar "hole" of our own? In Genesis we read the story of Joseph being thrown into the pit by his brothers. "The pit was empty; there was no water in it" (Gen. 37:24 NKJV). Despair is also empty, dark, isolating, and void of nourishment.

Job suffered so greatly that his wife suggested he "curse God and die!" (Job 2:9).

Though the prophet Elijah fled to a mountaintop after his exhausting fight with the prophets of Baal, he found himself in an emotional and spiritual pit. "'I have had enough, LORD,' he said. 'Take my life'" (1 Kings 19:4). But that wasn't God's plan. Twice he sent an angel to bring food and drink to Elijah, saying, "Get up and eat, for the journey is too much for you" (v. 7).

The journey is too much for you. The Lord knows this. He did not ridicule or minimize Elijah's desperation, and he doesn't do that to us, either. May we cry to God for help, as David did: "Do not let the floodwaters engulf me or the depths swallow me up or the pit close its mouth over me" (Ps. 69:15).

For God is mighty to save (Ps. 40:2). Though he allows us to experience the pit, and we must work through our grief, he does not desire that we dwell there permanently.

That day Ellen learned Nichole could die, she searched her heart. "Could I live knowing I held back from loving my baby because she was not what I had expected, not what I wanted?" She pulled herself to her knees, stretched out her arms to God and cried, "'I choose love, Lord! From this day on, with everything that is within me, I choose love!' And God pulled me out of the hole, and held me in his arms. Because he had chosen love for me too."[6]

That was several years ago. While Ellen remembers that scare as the moment God pulled her up out of her pit, her life has not been grief-free ever since. She loves Nichole fiercely. Still, grief rolls in and out like an irregular tide, with new medical complications, difficult IEP meetings, missed milestones, and even memories. In her memoir *Sun Shine Down*, Gillian Marchenko shares that when her daughter with Down syndrome was twenty-one months old, "Grief packed up his bags and told me he was going hitchhiking across the country, though he promised to send postcards."[7]

No matter how many times we slip into grief, God does not scold us for being there. Gently, lovingly, he offers his hand. His message to Elijah he says to us as well: *I know the journey is too much for you. Let me help you up and nourish you with living water.*

Lord, help me learn how to grieve my losses in healthy ways. Thank you that I don't need to hide my grief from you. Help me up out of the pit, and give me a firm place to stand. In Jesus's name, amen.

DIGGING DEEPER
1. When was the last time you felt stuck in a pit?
2. What most helped you to climb out?
3. Next time you slip into a pit, how do you hope to handle it?

THROUGH WATERS DEEP

Kimberly

But now, this is what the LORD says—he who created you,
Jacob, he who formed you, Israel: "Do not fear, for I have
redeemed you; I have summoned you by name; you are
mine. When you pass through the waters, I will be with
you; and when you pass through the rivers, they will not
sweep over you. When you walk through the fire, you
will not be burned; the flames will not set you ablaze."

ISAIAH 43:1-2

Almost immediately after being discharged from the NICU, Abbey began to receive early intervention services. Suddenly complete strangers were in my home, touching my baby and telling me how to care for her, five days a week. These were in addition to all the specialists and physicians who were now on our speed dial. It was a dramatically different routine than I'd expected. Into the calendar went many appointments: OT, PT, speech therapy, developmental therapist, doctors, and clinics. Out went family time, friend time, me time, and church time. By the time Abbey reached the age of three, I thought there was a good chance I would never have the gift of a friend, the blessing of a healthy marriage, or the joy of other children.

I couldn't have been more wrong.

In those trials and early years, I learned so much about the character of God, my sinful nature, and the hope I have in him. When our routines and our child's disabilities threaten us, we have to hold on to the promises in Scripture passages such as Isaiah 43:1–2. We will pass through the waters; the waters are unavoidable, but we are never alone. God promises that with him by our side, they will not destroy us.

Sometimes these waters show us the depth of our own sinful nature. As I found my marriage struggling with our new normal, I turned to other friendships for comfort and assurance. Ryan turned to his new job and spent many hours beyond what was necessary away from home in order to gain a sense of control over our out-of-control life. A deep wedge was forming between us. When family and circumstances opened our eyes to our situation, we knew that God could use this to refine us. We turned to Isaiah 48:10–11 as a verse for our marriage: "See, I have refined you, though not as silver; I have tested you in the furnace of affliction. For my own sake, for my own sake, I do this. How can I let myself be defamed? I will not yield my glory to another."

We need to know we're not alone. We need to allow what we are going through to refine us, and yet it's also exciting to learn new things about our relationship with the living God, for his glory. Jared Buckley, whose daughter Fayth has Down syndrome, explains on his blog:

> We have learned that through the power of Jesus Christ, there is nothing we cannot handle. We have given our worries, concerns, fears, anxieties, and struggles over to Jesus and have come out victorious (Romans 8:34–39). We live our life encouraged, hopeful, peaceful, and joyful because our life is not our own and we live by faith in Jesus Christ (Galatians 2:20). We are now co-heirs to Christ's throne and live in His kingdom and presence everyday (Romans 8:17).
>
> There is nothing that can take away our victory through

Jesus. This victory has given us the greatest peace in our parenting a special needs child. When all things happen, we come
back to the fact that Jesus still reigns and He has and will
always love us unconditionally. [The] result is encouragement.[8]

Sometimes the new normal is excruciatingly difficult, yes, but it can
also be amazingly beautiful. There will be days when it feels like it's all
you can do to keep your head above water. But not only is God with
you, he also will lead you through until you're safe on the other side.

*Dear Jesus, I praise you that you promise I don't have to do this
alone. Use this new normal to show me the depth of your love, to
refine my character, and to teach me about yours. In Jesus's name,
amen.*

Digging Deeper

1. What areas of your new normal are difficult to manage?
2. In what ways can you see God refining you through this process?
3. How has your refining process shown you new discoveries about
   God's character?

NOT READY TO CELEBRATE

Jocelyn

How long must I wrestle with my thoughts and
day after day have sorrow in my heart?

PSALM 13:2

I'm not ready for this, Laura Slezak thought as she pushed her three-year-old son in the stroller beneath the Florida sun. Beside her, her husband, Craig, pushed their one-year-old daughter Ava, who was recently diagnosed with Angelman syndrome, a complex genetic disorder that includes delayed development, intellectual disability, severe speech impairment, problems with movement and balance, and seizures. Surrounding them were other parents and children with Angelman's, and supportive friends and family. They were participating in the national walk for the Angelman Syndrome Foundation.

Laura was overwhelmed at the sight of so many older kids with the syndrome all in one place. "One woman told me that she couldn't believe I was even at the walk, because she had refused to participate soon after her child had been diagnosed," Laura recalled. "That was so reassuring to me, because I was totally hating being at the walk at that point and wished I hadn't gone. I needed to know that other moms probably felt the same way at first and that I'm not crazy or a bad mom for being depressed."

Another dad told Laura the first two years were the hardest for him, but that it did get better. It was exactly what she needed to hear. "So, it's OK if I'm not OK with this for another year, even if everyone else thinks that's a ridiculously long time," Laura said.

Even the most steadfast believers are allowed to own their sorrow. David, a man after God's own heart (1 Sam. 13:14), expressed grief and dismay in his psalms. Most of his laments reveal that he felt God had deliberately withdrawn his loving protection:

How long, LORD? Will you forget me forever? How long will you hide your face from me? How long must I wrestle with my thoughts and day after day have sorrow in my heart? (Ps. 13:1–2)

My tears have been my food day and night, while people say to me all day long, "Where is your God?" (Ps. 42:3)

I am worn out calling for help; my throat is parched. My eyes fail, looking for my God. (Ps. 69:3)

When Jacob saw his son Joseph's bloodied and shredded robe, he assumed Joseph was dead. "All his sons and daughters came to comfort him, but he refused to be comforted. 'No,' he said, 'I will continue to mourn *until I join my son in the grave*.' So his father wept for him" (Gen. 37:35, emphasis added). If this hero of the faith did not give his grief a tight deadline, you don't need to either.

Mourning a loss of any kind is normal and necessary. When parents learn of their child's diagnosis, they mourn the child and the future they were expecting to have. "It's a slow process of adjusting my heart and mind to what IS rather than holding on to what I wanted," Laura wrote. "I know the more I adjust to and accept reality, the more I will be able to see the good things and the joy God is holding for us in the midst of it."[9]

In the first year or two of your child's diagnosis, it may be impossible to imagine feeling any better than you do now. Allow other parents who are further down the road to give you hope. Like David, you'll be able to end your lament with trust in God's love (Ps. 13:5) and with hope in him (Ps. 42:11). But in the meantime, it's OK if you're not ready to celebrate.

> *Lord, thank you for allowing me to grieve without guilt. Help me process this in healthy ways. Please help my spouse and me to be compassionate toward one another, as we may handle our pain in different ways. Bring me to the other side of this grief, as you brought David through his. In Jesus's name, amen.*

DIGGING DEEPER

1. Do you feel guilty about how long you've been grieving? If so, why?
2. What is one healthy way you can work through your grief?
3. Can you identify something you should avoid because it only makes you feel worse?

COPING

Kimberly

> Moses' father-in-law replied, "What you are doing
> is not good. You and these people who come to you will only
> wear yourselves out. The work is too heavy for you;
> you cannot handle it alone."
>
> EXODUS 18:17-18

I wasn't even sure how it happened. But the truth glared up at me from my bathroom scale. I had gained one hundred pounds in the first year of my daughter's life. Instead of turning to God to help me deal with the strain of serving a child with multiple disabilities, I had turned to sleep and food.

We all find ways to cope. Unfortunately, not every method is healthy. Gillian Marchenko turned to alcohol after her baby was born with Down syndrome. "It wasn't long before I was drinking a bottle of wine at night. It helped me sleep." She found herself wanting alcohol even earlier in the day, and even describes being hung over at an 11:00 a.m. church service. "While fighting the urge to puke, I bowed my head during prayer like everyone else. But I could not pray, because my head was still spinning. *Oh my gosh! Am I drunk in church?*"[10] It was a turning point for Gillian, after which she deliberately turned to healthier ways to cope.

Jeff Davidson, whose son has autism and cerebral palsy, coped by accumulating possessions. "I put in a pool, bought a hot tub, drove the nicest SUVs, and remodeled our house. I traded cars every year and a half, and I tried to spend us out of the pain. I hit rock bottom when I converted half our basement into a man cave. . . . One night [I realized what I'd done]. Going down into the basement meant going down fifteen narrow steps to get there. My son, with his cerebral palsy, would never be able to come down there. Jon Alex would never be able to join me in my man cave. I realized I had built a monument to my own selfishness, greed, and needs."[11]

Did any of us intentionally decide to adopt a harmful habit? No. The danger lies in the fact that we don't have to. At every turn, the world will offer us coping mechanisms to deal with our pain. It is far easier to slip into any of them than it is to resist. We must realize, however, that what we need is more of Christ in our lives, in our days, in our messy moments. We don't need more alcohol, or more ice cream, or more shoes, or more technology. Those things won't heal us. Christ will. "The one who is in you is greater than the one who is in the world" (1 John 4:4).

In addition to turning to Christ to overcome, we can also look for help from an accountability partner or support group. In Exodus 18, Moses found himself becoming worn out from judging the disputes brought before him from morning until evening. Wisely, his father-in-law told him in verse 22 to share the burden with others in order to make the load lighter. Ecclesiastes 4 tells us that two are better than one (v. 9), and a cord of three strands is not quickly broken (v. 12).

When we turn to Christ and to Christian supporters, we find the strength to fight the battle of our unhealthy coping mechanisms. Over the last fourteen years, the Lord has worked in my heart to heal my grief in stages, and he continues to transform my mind to be more like his. The work he has done in my spirit has translated to a sixty-pound weight loss on my body. I still struggle with food and the desire to sleep instead of dealing with the issues at hand, but I am encouraged that he who began a good work in me will be faithful to complete it (Phil. 1:6).

Dear Lord, you are mercy and forgiveness. Help me turn from harmful habits and look to you instead. Give me the strength to reach out to others for help. In Jesus's name, amen.

Digging Deeper

1. Are there any unhealthy coping mechanisms that you are currently using to deal with your pain? If so, what are they?
2. What can you do to no longer turn to things rather than to Christ for healing and comfort?
3. With whom can you share your story for accountability and prayer?

YEAR OF FEAR

Jocelyn

Be alert and of sober mind. Your enemy the devil prowls
around like a roaring lion looking for someone to devour.

1 PETER 5:8

While her husband was deployed with the National Guard, Rebekah Benimoff's four-year-old son was diagnosed with type one diabetes. What they didn't know at the time was that little Tyler also had sensory processing issues, making the necessary insulin shots truly traumatic.

In the coming months, Rebekah put her grief on hold as she tried desperately to "conquer" diabetes, all the while consumed with fear that her son would die. With her husband away, she, Tyler, and her one-year-old son Blaine moved in with her parents. Rebekah checked Tyler's blood sugar six to eight times a day, counted his carbs, and administered the shots while her mother held down her hysterical son.

For much of that year, terror hounded Rebekah as Tyler suffered multiple seizures and episodes of incoherence. And once the little boy realized that shots came with food, he refused to eat. "I was pounded with fears for my son's life with each fight over a meal, each blood glucose test, each low blood glucose incident," Rebekah said. "The enemy was having a heyday at my expense. I was allowing my fear to pull me away from the very One who could have helped me through such a difficult season. And so I bought into the lie that I was alone and became paralyzed by fear."

Most likely you can relate. Especially during the "diagnosis year," there are many adjustments and unknowns to deal with, not to mention a tangle of emotions to work through. Just as Eve believed Satan when she was alone with him in the garden of Eden, we are vulnerable to believing the Great Deceiver when we are alone with our fears. Be aware of this tactic! Don't be fooled. You are not alone. "The LORD himself goes before you and will be with you; he will never leave you nor forsake you. Do not be afraid; do not be discouraged" (Deut. 31:8).

When Satan whispers to your soul that God doesn't care what you're going through, combat that lie with the truth: "Cast all your anxiety on him *because he cares for you*" (1 Peter 5:7, emphasis added). The very next verse warns us, "Be alert and of sober mind. Your enemy the devil prowls around like a roaring lion looking for someone to devour." I believe these two verses are side by side for a reason. When we tell God how we really feel, allow him to shoulder our burden, and believe that he is intimately concerned with our lives, we are better able to be alert to our prowling enemy.

Don't be shy about asking a trusted friend to pray for you too. As Rebekah said, "You do not have to 'deal' with fear; instead, wage war." And in any battle, it would be foolhardy not to call for reinforcements when you need them. Seek out support, whether it's your church, your family, friends, an online group, your pastor, or a counselor.

Fear can either drive us away from the Lord or bring us to our knees. Next time you feel assaulted by fear, fight back, and know that you are not battling alone. "Be strong and courageous. Do not be frightened, and do not be dismayed, for the LORD your God is with you wherever you go" (Josh. 1:9 ESV).

Lord, give me strength and courage. Remind me hourly that you are with me, and guide me to the right people you've already chosen to help me walk through this. Help me deflect each of Satan's lies with your truths. Unshackle me from fear. In Jesus's name, amen.

DIGGING DEEPER

1. When you're afraid, what do you tend to do?
2. The last time you were afraid, did you move toward or away from God? How?
3. What was the underlying belief that caused you to respond that way?

IDENTITY

Kimberly

For we are God's handiwork, created in Christ Jesus to do
good works, which God prepared in advance for us to do.

EPHESIANS 2:10

Who am I? This is a question I ask myself on a fairly regular basis.
When I am lost in doctors' appointments, medical bills, and
the daily grind of caring for someone with special needs, I often think,
"There just has to be more to me than this!" And there is. There is so
much more. If I'm being honest, though, sometimes it can feel like my
identity is swallowed up in caring for my daughter.

Shannon McNeil understands this all too well. She shared, "Even
though I know I can work to make things different, my identity has
morphed into [my children's]. I am caretaker, therapist, nurse, insurance manager, chef, bathroom attendant, laundress, etc. I spend most
of my time making sure they are well cared for and loved. I am realizing that I have been solely identifying myself as the mother of Waverly
and Oliver who have Sanfilippo syndrome. And while I love being their
mother and caring for their every need, I have to cultivate me."[12]

Cultivating who we are means understanding that being the parent
of a child with special needs is just one part of us.

To begin with, if you're a fellow believer, we are first and forever children of God because of what Christ did for us on the cross. "Now if we are children, then we are heirs—heirs of God and co-heirs with Christ, if indeed we share in his sufferings in order that we may also share in his glory" (Rom. 8:17). Not only so, but "in all these things we are more than conquerors through him who loved us. For I am convinced that neither death nor life, neither angels nor demons, neither the present nor the future, nor any powers, neither height nor depth, nor anything else in all creation, will be able to separate us from the love of God that is in Christ Jesus our Lord" (vv. 37–39). I love those verses! We are not just conquerors in all these things; we are even *more*.

First Corinthians 12 discusses our unique spiritual gifts and how each of us is a deeply unique and needed part of the body of Christ. I encourage you to read through this entire chapter and ask God to show you the gifts he has given you. One way to quickly get out of the mind-set of a caregiver identity is to serve in an area of the church completely unrelated to that role. Be a greeter, sing in the choir, fold bulletins, clean up chairs, make meals, write encouraging notes—do whatever your energy and time will allow. Serving a role in the church body is both uplifting and affirming.

Spend some time reading through Psalm 139 as well. It is a beautiful picture of the thought and tenderness that God put into creating not only our children but us as well. We were planned. Not only that, but Ephesians 2:10 assures us that we were planned with a purpose in mind.

With these truths firmly in place, may we make the time to be more fully who God created us to be. Sometimes that means going to a lot of work to have our children cared for so we can have time to do something else, whether it's ministry, work, or self-care. When we take the time to connect with God and with others, we remember that we are more than caregiving parents. We are children of God. We are more than conquerors, and dearly loved. We are each uniquely gifted and enabled to serve the body of Christ in a role that, no matter how small, is truly needed. We were created with a purpose.

Father God, you know my name. I'm written on the palm of your hands. Help me to see myself through your eyes and to have the courage to explore all you've created me to be and do for your glory. In Jesus's name, amen.

Digging Deeper

1. What are other pieces to your identity, besides caregiver, that you've been missing?
2. What is one small way you can try to be more "you" this week?
3. What gifts do you think God gave you, and how can you better use them to serve him?

UNWELCOME CHANGES

Kimberly

Jesus Christ is the same yesterday
and today and forever.
HEBREWS 13:8

When Abbey turned thirteen, I could no longer ignore the fact that my little girl was growing into a woman. I truly cannot believe how fast these years have gone. I think for most people, having teenagers comes with a little fear and trepidation, but for us, puberty has definitely brought some unwelcome changes. Taking care of the physical needs of a cute little four-year-old with ringlets is nothing at all like changing a diaper on your teenage daughter.

Just when we thought we had figured out how to care for our child, everything changed. We went from lots of babysitters to just a few who are willing to change Abbey. We went from controllable outbursts to a body almost my height and impossible to discretely carry out of the grocery store. Just when I think I've got this figured out, I find myself reeling and looking for something to hold on to.

While our circumstances are changing, Christ's love stands firm. "I will sing of the LORD's great love forever; with my mouth I will make your faithfulness known through all generations. I will declare that your love stands firm forever, that you have established your faithfulness in heaven itself" (Ps. 89:1–2).

The landscape of caring for our children will continue to shift and move, and it can feel overwhelming. It's important to remember, when we receive a new diagnosis or the care of our child changes, that while our world seems to be spinning out of control, God is in complete control. He is unchangeable. In Revelation 22:13 God speaks: "I am the Alpha and the Omega, the First and the Last, the Beginning and the End."

From the beginning of creation, the Alpha and Omega had a plan to resolve and redeem. No matter what dark circumstances you are facing, have peace knowing that the light of Christ's life has overcome it.

We can find strength knowing that we *belong* to the same God who both created and overcame this world. "He tends his flock like a shepherd: He gathers the lambs in his arms and carries them close to his heart; he gently leads those that have young" (Isa. 40:11). As the parent of a fragile child, this verse has always given me great comfort. It's not just our children whom God cares for as his precious lambs. He loves us, the parents, in the exact same way. God knows our weaknesses, how fragile we are compared to his greatness, and he gathers us in his arms. He carries us close to his heart and gently leads us as we take care of these special children.

Whether you are dealing with a new diagnosis, a new set of complications, or a new stage of life with its own challenges and learning curves, take heart, dear friend. God will see you through these unwelcome changes; may you find hope in his unchanging character as he does.

Dear Lord, I praise you because you are the same yesterday, today, and forever. I find my hope in your unchanging character. Help me to hold on to these promises as I navigate my child's special needs. In Jesus's name, amen.

DIGGING DEEPER

1. What has changed in your life recently as the result of your child with special needs?
2. If you can, find and list several Scripture verses to encourage you through these changes.
3. How does it make you feel to know that although your life will change, God himself does not change?

THE INTERPRETER

Kimberly

In the same way, the Spirit helps us in our weakness.
We do not know what we ought to pray for,
but the Spirit himself intercedes for us through wordless
groans. And he who searches our hearts knows the mind
of the Spirit, because the Spirit intercedes for God's people
in accordance with the will of God.

ROMANS 8:26-27

When our youngest son was three, he discovered that Abbey couldn't talk. Cooper would stop and watch her and then turn and say matter-of-factly, "Abbey is disabled; she can't talk." As it did with his other brother, the reality of Abbey's disability was starting to sink in for Cooper. He was quick to begin speaking for her, saying things like, "Abbey wants some chocolate milk, and me too!" or "Abbey wants a movie." The compassion and empathy he has for her are growing more every day. Despite her lack of words, Abbey has grown to trust all of us to interpret what she needs, wants, and feels on a moment-by-moment basis. Every day of her life will be spent leaning on the capable mind and voice of someone else to speak and act on her behalf.

I don't know about you, but there are times in my life when there just aren't words to describe what I'm feeling, and my prayers feel like they are so empty. It's in those times that I'm encouraged by Abbey to learn to trust the capable mind and voice of the Father God who is always acting on my behalf. Romans 8:26–27 assures us that the Spirit himself searches our hearts and will interpret our needs to the Father.

The Spirit also gives us godly wisdom. First Corinthians 2:10–13 explains:

> These are the things God has revealed to us by his Spirit.
>
> The Spirit searches all things, even the deep things of God. For who knows a person's thoughts except their own spirit within them? In the same way no one knows the thoughts of God except the Spirit of God. What we have received is not the spirit of the world, but the Spirit who is from God, so that we may understand what God has freely given us. This is what we speak, not in words taught us by human wisdom but in words taught by the Spirit, explaining spiritual realities with Spirit-taught words.

As we trust the Spirit to intercede on our behalf, we can also trust the things taught by the Spirit through God's Word to guide us. "Trust in the LORD with all your heart and lean not on your own understanding; in all your ways submit to him, and he will make your paths straight" (Prov. 3:5–6).

In her Bible study *Walking by Faith: Lessons Learned in the Dark*, Jennifer Rothschild shares spiritual lessons she has learned as a result of becoming blind from a rare degenerative eye disease. She wrote, "We never learn whether someone is worthy of our trust unless we risk walking with him—and that's what God invites us to do. 'Oh, taste and see that the LORD is good,' David says, 'blessed is the man who trusts in Him!' (Ps. 34:8 NKJV)."[13]

We can follow Christ in full confidence, knowing he will lead us safely down a straight path to himself. The psalmist calls out, "Since you are my rock and my fortress, for the sake of your name lead and guide me" (Ps. 31:3).

The Spirit sees our hearts with compassion and empathy, and he goes to the Father to intercede for us. May we learn how to trust that the Spirit of God sees our weakness and knows how to interpret what we can't find the words to say. He gives godly wisdom and is a trustworthy guide. Every day of our life can be spent leaning on the capable mind and voice of the One who speaks and acts on our behalf.

Dear Lord, I thank you for the Spirit who intercedes for me when I don't know what to pray. You alone search and know my heart. I trust you to lead me. In Jesus's name, amen.

DIGGING DEEPER

1. What was happening the last time you didn't know what to pray?
2. How does it comfort you to know that in those wordless times, the Spirit intercedes for you?
3. In what areas of your life do you need to stop taking the lead and instead ask Christ to guide you?

TWO

Sowing Seeds
Cultivating Truth and Faith

Remember this: Whoever sows sparingly
will also reap sparingly, and whoever sows
generously will also reap generously.

2 CORINTHIANS 9:6

TRUST DESPITE TROUBLES

Jocelyn

A furious squall came up, and the waves broke over the
boat, so that it was nearly swamped. Jesus was in the
stern, sleeping on a cushion. The disciples woke him and
said to him, "Teacher, don't you care if we drown?"

MARK 4:37-38

As Ellen Stumbo sat listening to her pastor and husband, Andy,
one morning in church, his words penetrated to a raw spot in her
heart. "Trusting in God in the midst of trial does not mean everything
will work out," he preached. "It means that by trusting we have peace,
even if the worst-case scenario happens."[1]

Ellen shuddered.

"The last two months have wrecked me," she explained on her blog.
The Stumbos' middle daughter, eight years old at the time, was adopted
from Ukraine when she was almost four. She has cerebral palsy, trauma
and attachment issues, and anxiety and depression. "I want to say,
'Everything is supposed to be getting better. She's supposed to allow
the love of a family to heal her heart, to feel God's love through us and
allow that love to undo all the damage caused by the trauma and pain
and loss she experienced those first four years of her life. She's supposed

to not let her physical limitations get her down because she knows we are her biggest cheerleaders and we got her back. She's supposed to leave that behind her and we all move on!'"

Two months of intense intervention, different medications, extra therapy, and loads of prayer, and things did improve. But Ellen can't help but fear the next time her daughter's hopelessness rages out of control.

"I want to trust God, but I want it to mean this is all behind us," she confessed. "However, God never promised to take our problems away, he did not promise prosperity and blissful joy. He promised trials, because life is messy."

In the gospel of Mark, we read the story of Jesus sleeping in the boat during a storm. The boat was taking on water, and the disciples were terrified. They woke Jesus with a question: "Teacher, don't you care if we drown?" (Mark 4:38). Not only did they assume they would not survive, but they accused Jesus of apathy. It's easy to relate to these sentiments, isn't it?

But Jesus was in the boat with the disciples throughout the storm. He himself had chosen the destination and the way to get there. In essence, he was the one who had put the disciples in what seemed to be harm's way.

In our own lives, we may be battered and rocked by storms. But may we always remember that Jesus is in the boat with us! He plotted our course, he brought us here, and he will never bail on us. The fact that he is unsurprised and unafraid of our storms does not mean he doesn't care about us. His love for his children knows no bounds.

In the story in Mark 4, Jesus rebuked the storm and it calmed. But God's response to storms is not always to quiet them when we ask. The apostles trusted in God completely, and they were martyred for their faith. Sometimes God may still the storm in your heart even though the waves of circumstance continue to batter your boat. When God says, "Peace! Be still!" (Mark 4:39 ESV), he may be speaking not to our situation, but to us. "And the peace of God, which transcends all understanding, will guard your hearts and your minds in Christ Jesus" (Phil. 4:7).

"It is a peace that is not dependent on circumstances, on whether our life is going well or falling apart," wrote Ellen. "And that is exactly the peace I want, the peace I need."

Lord, you are trustworthy. Teach me to trust you no matter what. Please fill me with your peace. Let me not be drowned in my storms. Thank you for being with me. In Jesus's name, amen.

DIGGING DEEPER
1. When have you struggled with trusting God most?
2. If God's peace guards your heart and mind, how would your day and life change?
3. How has God calmed your spirit even in the midst of a trial?

SEARCHING FOR PEACE

Kimberly

Peace I leave with you; my peace I give to you. Not
as the world gives do I give to you. Let not your
hearts be troubled, neither let them be afraid.
JOHN 14:27 (ESV)

Hospitals. It's amazing the emotions that one word can drag up!
When our daughter started her first year of pre-K, she was hospitalized three times in two months. Her little immune system just couldn't fight off all of those microscopic intruders. We rushed to the hospital each time with a sense of desperate urgency. There is nothing more terrifying than holding a limp child in your arms. She had a pale face, a lifeless body, and no strength to cry despite the poking and prodding of needles. I laid in the hospital bed next to her, my face wet from a relentless flow of quiet tears. Feeling helpless and afraid, I had a throbbing need to know that she was going to be OK.

So, where do we go when our hearts are troubled and afraid? In John 14:27, Jesus is sharing some final words with his disciples before the crucifixion. I have often imagined the emotional intensity of those moments in the upper room. These are Christ's beloved disciples who've dropped everything to follow him. He's about to face an agonizing death and temporary separation from God the Father. I'm sure the inner turmoil we see in the garden of Gethsemane is already starting to build as he has just dismissed Judas as his betrayer. In those crucial final moments he offers these gentle words: "Peace I leave with you; my peace I give to you. . . . Let not your hearts be troubled, neither let them be afraid" (ESV). He goes on to say in John 16:33, "I have said these things to you, that in me you may have peace. In the world you will have tribulation. But take heart; I have overcome the world" (ESV).

There is a simple and unavoidable fact here from Jesus himself. We *will* have tribulation in this world. If you look up tribulation in a thesaurus, you will find words such as *misfortune, trial, suffering, pain, distress,* and *trouble.* In my own life, I can relate each of those words to the word *hospital.* But when I find myself in tribulation, I have to run to Jesus. His words of affirmation and his love to his disciples are also his gift to me. I have the peace that comes from a saving knowledge of Jesus. I know that this earthly life is not the end of the story, praise God! The world can offer me nothing that more deeply satisfies and comforts than to be in Christ and the promise of what awaits me and my little girl in eternity. Jesus has overcome the world, and my hope in him is my great reward and my lasting peace.

If you find yourself feeling helpless, troubled, and afraid, then recall the words of Christ. Say them out loud and let them find a home in your heart. He says, "In me you may have peace."

Dear Jesus, I know that at times I will feel helpless and afraid, but I also know that you have overcome the world. Help me to run to you when I feel this way and not to settle for the counterfeit peace that the world offers. Thank you for what you did for me on the cross. Thank you for leaving your Spirit to intercede on my behalf, and for being my perfect peace. I know I am safe with you. In Jesus's name, amen.

DIGGING DEEPER

1. When was the last time you needed to feel God's peace?
2. From which sources, other than God, do you sometimes seek peace? When you do that, how do you feel?
3. How does keeping an eternal perspective help you cope with daily trials?

LIFELINE THEOLOGY

Jocelyn

I form the light and create darkness, I bring prosperity
and create disaster; I, the LORD, do all these things.

ISAIAH 45:7

Jill Solomon was a healthy baby until her first seizures began at the
age of three months. By the time she was one, she suffered multiple
major seizures every day. On her first Thanksgiving, she had nineteen
grand mal seizures. When she was eight years old, a rash of them left her
without the ability to walk, stand, and sit in a chair on her own.

That was more than fifteen years ago. Mitochondrial disease, from
which Jill suffers, is progressive, incurable, and causes debilitating physical, developmental, and cognitive disabilities including loss of muscle
coordination, muscle weakness and pain, seizures, vision and/or hearing
loss, gastrointestinal issues, learning disabilities, and organ failure. To
date, this young woman has had close to six thousand seizures, leaving
her severely mentally disabled. Treatments have allowed her to regain
all of her mobility, but she has lost her speech, is not potty trained, and
cannot dress herself. She has no concept of danger, so someone must
watch her every moment.

Jill's disease put an incredible strain on Lon and Brenda Solomon's marriage, stole countless hours of their sleep, and heaped guilt upon them for not being as present with their three older sons as with Jill.

"In the early years, the immensity of Jill's disabilities and mental retardation were often overwhelming," Lon wrote in his book, *Brokenness*. "Brenda and I nearly gave up. We had hardly any hope in a medical solution, little joy in our lives, and we began to believe there was no way out of the bleak situation we were in."[2] It would have been easy to become bitter and cynical, wrote Lon, pastor of McLean Bible Church in McLean, Virginia.

Their lifeline was the conviction that God was personally involved with all that was happening to them. First, they believe that far from being an accident, God was making the final choices about Jill's condition and all that was happening with her. In Job chapters 1 and 2, it's clear that Satan could do nothing to Job without the Lord's express permission and limitations. Job saw God as the ultimate source of what was happening to him. "Shall we accept good from God, and not trouble?" (Job 2:10). To believe that Satan inflicted suffering beyond God's control would be to credit Satan with more power than God, who would then cease to be God at all.

Second, the Solomons believe God has a plan into which all of this suffering fits: "We know that in all things God works for the good of those who love him, who have been called according to his purpose" (Rom. 8:28). Lon and Brenda have seen this verse come true in their lives, as God used their brokenness for good (see "Jill's House," p. 262).

Finally, the Solomons believe God has a purpose for their pain (Ps. 138:8 ESV)—even though they have no idea what that might be. "'For my thoughts are not your thoughts, neither are your ways my ways,' declares the LORD" (Isa. 55:8). Life was still hard, but these truths gave them the confidence they needed to press on in the journey.

It may be tempting to say that theology makes no difference, practically speaking, in the real world. But what we believe about who God says he is makes *all* the difference. It is the difference between meaningful and meaningless, hopeful and hopeless, faithful and faithless. If you haven't yet done so today, crack open your Bible. Find a verse mentioned in this devotional and read the surrounding chapter. Or look up a word in the concordance and study several Scriptures on the same topic. God's Word is a lamp to our feet and a light to our path (Ps. 119:105). Our theology matters, every day.

Lord, your ways are not my ways. But I trust you to redeem all that we've been through for our good and for your glory. When I falter, bring me back to the truths of your Word. Give me a hunger to know you more, and a thirst for your Scriptures. Be my lifeline, Lord. In Jesus's name, amen.

DIGGING DEEPER

1. When you consider that God is involved in what's happening in your family, how do you feel?
2. Which verse from today's reading strikes you the most? Why?
3. What is one way you can spend a little more time reading the Bible?

LONGING FOR TRANSFORMATION

Kimberly

Do not be conformed to this world, but be
transformed by the renewal of your mind, that by
testing you may discern what is the will of God,
what is good and acceptable and perfect.

ROMANS 12:2 (ESV)

Getting my daughter dressed every morning includes fitting her legs into orthopedic braces which force her limbs into an uncomfortable position. Those braces fight a daily battle against what the cerebral palsy tells her little body to do. The goal is to stretch and loosen the tightness in the legs, allowing her to walk properly. The constant stretching is supposed to help with the overall tightness by keeping her legs from going back to their natural muscle tone.

But Abbey's sickness isn't in her legs—it's damage done in her brain for which there is no repair apart from God's miraculous healing. When I put on her braces in the morning, I recognize the symbolism of forcing her body to do something that is only a temporary solution to her problem. It is exactly what is happening in my own life at times: I am trying to "force" myself to do the right things to honor God.

It's not a bad thing to want to be more like Christ, but doing good out of obligation is only a temporary solution to a depraved mind. What I really need is spiritual transformation, possible only through the miraculous work of the Holy Spirit living in me. Apart from him, there is nothing I can do to treat my sickness that will have any permanent effect.

The tense for the verb "transformed" in Romans 12:2 implies that it is not a onetime thing, but a process of being continually transformed. Its Greek word, *metamorphousthe*, in English is "metamorphosis." To be metamorphosed into something completely new, I have to *want* to be changed. I have to connect to the God who changes me, owns me, and loves me.

The process of peeling myself away from the patterns of this world is often painful and uncomfortable, just like Abbey's legs being forced to do what feels unnatural to her body. Through the power of the Holy Spirit, I continually renew my mind in Christ. The result: pleasing God, which was once forced, becomes more natural because of the Spirit's work of transformation in my heart and soul. I read and meditate on his Word, spend time in prayer, and fellowship with other believers. I begin to see life through a biblical, God-centered perspective rather than through my own self-tinted lens. This transformation in my life brings him glory. As others see the Lord working in me and changing me, I can give testimony to Christ in my life.

As we watch and help our children endure pain to improve physically, let it be a reminder that beyond physical healing, true spiritual healing can be claimed in Christ as we are transformed by the renewing of our minds.

Dear Lord, help me to be truly transformed by the renewing of my mind. It's the only way that I can have lasting change and not conform to the patterns of this world. I thank you that I have your Holy Spirit working in me and that you promise to finish in me what you began by making me more like Christ. In Jesus's name, amen.

Digging Deeper

1. Name one area of your life in which you'd like to experience some transformation.
2. In what ways have you been transformed since your special child came into your life?
3. What area of your heart might God be trying to work on right now?

THE SACRIFICE OF PRAISE

Jocelyn

Through Jesus, therefore, let us continually
offer to God a sacrifice of praise—the fruit
of lips that openly profess his name.

HEBREWS 13:15

"Lots of Down syndrome babies with this type of heart defect don't make it," the doctor said, and offered abortion as a solution for the baby inside Alana Sankey. Alana said no. "This is our baby," she told them. "We are keeping her."

But what if it was God who decided to take the baby? As much as Alana hated to entertain that possibility, it was something she had to make peace with. "Even if she would have died, I had to believe he still loved us. I had to decide he was still worthy of our praise."

When Tonya Nash's son was diagnosed with autism, she was overwhelmed. Her husband, who had planned to be home for her birthday the previous day, had his deployment extended and wasn't able to be with her when she received the news. "I had a conflict in my faith, because I thought I could pray my way out of it and change wasn't happening," she said. "One day as I was praying, God said to me, 'If I don't heal him, will you still praise me?'" God did not take autism from her son. But Tonya has learned to embrace it and praise the Lord anyhow.

Jeff Davidson thought he had a long-standing agreement with God. Jeff would devote his life to caring for his son who has multiple disabilities. But Jeff needed to outlive his son. Twice in five years, Jeff lay dead on a hospital table for minutes before his heart revived. Twice, he felt, God had come far too close to breaking the deal.

After recovering from his most recent incident, anger, doubt, and fear assailed Jeff, especially at night. "In defiance, summoning all the courage I [could] feebly muster, I mutter[ed] like Job, 'Blessed be the name of the Lord. Shall we accept good from God and not trouble?'"[3]

Sometimes it's easy to praise the Lord. And sometimes it hurts.

When Alana, Tonya, and Jeff praised God despite their circumstances, they were truly offering a "sacrifice of praise."

A sacrifice is the surrender of one valuable thing for the sake of something else considered even more valuable. It's painful even though it's worth it. Job was in agony when he "fell to the ground in worship" and said, "The LORD gave and the LORD has taken away; may the name of the LORD be praised" (Job 1:20–21). The crucifixion was excruciating, even though both Jesus and God the Father knew that Jesus would rise again in three days.

Some days we can praise God with our own words despite our fears and trials. Other times, we must borrow the praise of another, as Jeff repeated Job's words, having none of his own to offer. When she's too angry to pray, Anne-Marie Wurzel, whose daughter suffered brain damage through a metabolic crisis, cranks up the praise music. It shifts her focus to God rather than her circumstances, she says, and reminds her that this life is temporary.

When we offer a sacrifice of praise, we may not be killing a snow-white lamb, but we are laying our personal hopes and plans on the altar. We are agreeing with God that he is worthy of praise and thanksgiving regardless of our circumstances. We are admitting that God's greatness has nothing to do with how we feel at the moment and everything to do with who he is. "Those who sacrifice thank offerings honor me" (Ps. 50:23).

Lord, give me the fortitude to say, Though my child suffers and my family is strained, though my life is not at all like I thought it would be, yet will I rejoice in you. You are the strength in every step I take. In Jesus's name, amen.

Digging Deeper
1. When do you find it easy to praise God?
2. When is it a sacrifice for you to praise or thank God?
3. Next time you don't have the words to praise God, which Scripture verse might you quote instead?

REMEMBERING MATTERS

Kimberly

I remember the days of long ago; I meditate on all your
works and consider what your hands have done.

PSALM 143:5

Sometimes the greatest joy can come from the smallest accomplish-
ment. Not that long ago, Abbey came home from school and went
right to the kitchen. She pulled out a yogurt from the fridge, went to the
drawer and got a spoon, and then sat down and started hitting the table
to get my attention. I thought I was going to pass out! She'd never done
anything like that before. I was completely amazed that she not only
recognized hunger but knew where to get food, what food she wanted,
that she needed a utensil, where to get it, that we eat at the table, and
that she needed my help. As many of you know, when your child doesn't
speak or communicate, you sometimes have no idea what's going on
inside his or her mind.

Abbey continues to surprise us in so many ways. The first time she
laid down in the tub to play and knew to keep her mouth out of the
water; the first time she asked for her hearing aids by pulling on my
shirt and touching her ears; the first time she signed "friend," and so
many other moments could easily be forgotten if they hadn't meant so

much to us. It's those small moments that keep us going when we're struggling through the list of milestones still not met. Those moments give us the strength to keep trying and fighting. No small victory goes unnoticed or uncelebrated.

Recalling God's goodness and faithfulness over the small, everyday things can sometimes give us the strength needed to wait on God through the more difficult trials we face. It's so important to recognize his hand at work in our lives. If we don't pay attention, we can miss so many ways he reaches out to us, answers us, and loves us. Opening our eyes, mind, and heart to seeing God's faithfulness, goodness, and love toward us keeps our hearts in a place of gratitude.

Having eyes to see and ears to hear is a spiritual analogy. If your child lacks either of those senses, as mine does, then you understand at an even deeper level how important they are and what the analogy really means. In Matthew 13:15–16, Jesus says, "'For this people's heart has become calloused; they hardly hear with their ears, and they have closed their eyes. Otherwise they might see with their eyes, hear with their ears, understand with their hearts and turn, and I would heal them.' But blessed are your eyes because they see, and your ears because they hear."

No matter how small it may seem, each time we experience God's hand in our lives, it must be noticed and celebrated. Recounting it to him will help us to hang on in our difficulty and also bring glory to God as we praise him and acknowledge all he's done for us. Psalm 77 shows a man crying out to see God's hand at work, and when it comes to him, he says, "I will remember the deeds of the LORD; yes, I will remember your miracles of long ago. I will consider all your works and meditate on all your mighty deeds" (vv. 11–12).

Lord, thank you for your great faithfulness. Give me eyes to see your goodness, ears to hear what you are saying to me, and a soft and open heart to respond to you. Don't let me forget you and all that you've done for me. Help me to remember these things when the demands of caring for my child overwhelm me and I feel discouraged. In Jesus's name, amen.

DIGGING DEEPER

1. Make a list of the most recent ways you have seen God's faithfulness in your life.
2. Do you think your spiritual eyes and ears are open and attentive to God? How can you tell?
3. How can your heart benefit from remembering God's goodness?

IT'S NOT OUR STORY

Jocelyn

"Neither this man nor his parents sinned,"
said Jesus, "but this happened so that the works
of God might be displayed in him."
JOHN 9:3

"How could this have happened?" Jeff Davidson wondered soon after his son's diagnosis. "Was God punishing us? Had we done something to cause his wrath?"[4]

The disciples posed a similar question: "Rabbi, who sinned, this man or his parents, that he was born blind?" Neither, Jesus told them. It wasn't a matter of punishment but of demonstrating God's glory. And then Jesus made the blind man see (John 9:1–7).

But physical healing is not always the path God chooses to glorify himself. When Paul pleaded for his thorn in the flesh to be healed, Jesus said, "My grace is sufficient for you, for my power is made perfect in weakness" (2 Cor. 12:9). God's power was displayed not by healing Paul but by sustaining him.

Time and again in Scripture, we see that glorifying God's name is the ultimate goal for both God and his Son. "For the sake of his great name the LORD will not reject his people" (1 Sam. 12:22). God is

69

glorified by caring for his people in ways that you and I can easily recognize. But he also uses pain and hardship to bring glory to his name. Jesus said,

> "Now my soul is troubled, and what shall I say? 'Father, save me from this hour'? No, it was for this very reason I came to this hour. Father, glorify your name!"
> Then a voice came from heaven, "I have glorified it, and will glorify it again." (John 12:27–28)

Glorifying God is our assignment as well (Matt. 5:16). Today, God is still writing his story in the hearts and lives of each of us. And just as it has been from the beginning of time, it's still about his glory.

Not that it's easy. "With everything Satan throws at us, the hardest thing to do is to remember that I am not in control, and there is a larger story happening that I am just a character in," said Rob Wurzel, whose daughter's metabolic crisis caused brain damage. "Somehow, someway all of this is going to honor and glorify God and further his kingdom and bring people to him. As much as I want things to be 'easy,' that isn't the path we are on—and that's OK."

Courtney Morrison, whose daughter was diagnosed with autism, said, "God has a purpose for this, a bigger purpose than anything I could see with my own human eyes. Having my faith and relationship with God has provided a great testimony to many friends." God has also lead Courtney to pursue a degree in special education, through which she prays God will use her for his glory in the lives of children and parents alike.

Jeff, too, has allowed his life to be changed by his son. What he began as worship services for special-needs families has grown into a national ministry called Rising Above, and an initiative for fathers of children with special needs called No More Vacant Dads. "The story of your life is really God's story," he wrote. "You are playing the role he has assigned to you. . . . Everything God does, he does to accomplish his purposes, and to bring glory and honor to his name. So my struggles become his stage. My trials become his triumphs. My weaknesses reveal his strengths. My responses show his glory."[5]

> *Lord, help me live my life in such a way that it brings glory to you. Use my family to display your power, your grace, and your strength. When I cannot see how our trials accomplish your purposes, sustain me so that I may still honor your name. In Jesus's name, amen.*

Digging Deeper

1. How does your attitude change when you think of your life as part of God's story?
2. When have you seen God glorified in a friend's life?
3. What can you do that would bring God glory?

UGLY TURNED BEAUTIFUL

Kimberly

[The Lord has sent me to] provide for those who
grieve in Zion—to bestow on them a crown of beauty
instead of ashes, the oil of joy instead of mourning,
and a garment of praise instead of a spirit of despair.
They will be called oaks of righteousness, a planting
of the Lord for thedisplay of his splendor.

ISAIAH 61:3

For almost three years, Abbey's hands have been covered with warts. We tried everything imaginable to get rid of them. What started out as a couple of warts eventually turned into many. Tiny warts were extremely visible and prominent on her hands; they became a major social problem, because one of Abbey's favorite things to do is to take someone by the hand and walk around together. As her mom, I didn't hesitate to hold her hands, but I saw other family members and her peer group at church slowly retreat from doing so. Abbey had trouble finding someone to let her hold their hand, and suddenly there was no one for her to walk around with. It broke my heart!

Last year we got invited to an exhibit at Abbey's school, where a group of disabled students were paired with artists using different mediums and techniques to create art. Abbey's name was next to a large sculpture made up of molded 3-D—you guessed it—hands. They were all different colors, in all different positions, and looked amazing presented together like that. We were filled with wonder as our family walked around the sculpture trying to find her hands. Excitement bubbled over when someone would point to one and say, "Here! This one is Abbey's hand!" They were easy to distinguish because of her warts. The exhibit was absolutely beautiful. Her visible flaws and brokenness were displayed in something people celebrated and admired.

This is what God is always in the process of doing with his people. He is the ultimate artist. No one but God can take something ruined, sad, empty, and lost and turn it into beauty, gladness, garments of praise, and the display of his splendor. Never forget that out of the ugliness of life, and even out of the difficulty of raising our children, God can work in a way that causes people to look intently at what's on display. They will walk around with wonder, and excitement will bubble over when they see the trademark of his hands at work. "Here! This one belongs to God," they will say. His work will be easy to distinguish because what once was filled with brokenness and sadness has been replaced with beauty. Philippians 1:6 states that we can be "confident of this, that he who began a good work in [us] will carry it on to completion until the day of Christ Jesus." This is a promise that God the Artist will not leave us in a back room as a pile of scraps! He intends to finish the work and set it up in his exhibit for display.

If you are dealing with something ugly in the care of your child, or if there is an ugly thing lurking in your life, heart, or mind today, I encourage you to give it to the Lord. His hands are capable of turning these ashes into something new and beautiful. Let your flaws and brokenness become a display of the Lord's splendor.

Father God, I praise and thank you that you make all things new and beautiful in your time. Help me to surrender my life and situation to your control. Give me confidence and hope that you can take not only my child's life but my own life as well into your hands and fashion ashes into beauty. You alone can replace despair with praise. Help my life, and my child's life, to be a display of your mighty splendor. In Jesus's name, amen.

DIGGING DEEPER

1. Are there any examples in your own life, or in the lives of people around you, where you have seen God turn something awful into something beautiful?

2. What is one "ugly" area of your life that you want to surrender to Christ today?

3. What does it mean to display the splendor of the Lord?

WHO KNOWS?

Kimberly

Behold, the LORD's hand is not shortened, that it
cannot save, or his ear dull, that it cannot hear.

ISAIAH 59:1 (ESV)

The difficult reality of a chronic illness or disability is that you find yourself often praying for the same things over and over. For the first year of my daughter's life, I went into her room while she slept, and several times a day I laid my hands on her body and asked the Lord to heal her. In some ways it became a routine. But despite the regularity of my prayers, I always felt a sense of sincere desperation as I stood over her, caressing her soft, baby-fine hair. At three months of age, she still didn't have that baby twinkle in her eyes that I knew she needed. I kept praying, and praying, and praying. Though she's gotten older and rarely naps, I still slip into her room and pray healing over her body while she rests.

I'm fully aware of the limitations of her disabilities and the severity of her brain damage. I'm also fully aware of the power and compassion of my great God. I wonder sometimes what illnesses she's been spared, complications avoided, and milestones unexpectedly met as the result of the many prayers over her. I will never know on this side of heaven.

I love the reminder in Isaiah 59:1 because of the tone of the verse. My ears always perk up when something begins with the word *behold*. When I see "behold," I sit up a little straighter in my seat and listen intently to the words I'm reading. Here God reminds us that he is not a lazy, unconcerned God. He's saying, "Listen up! Don't you see that I'm capable and that I hear you?" What greater solace can we have than the reassurance that not only does our magnificent Creator hear our prayers with his own ears, but his hand is also perfectly equipped to come to our aid.

First Thessalonians 5:16–18 says, "Rejoice always, pray continually, give thanks in all circumstances; for this is God's will for you in Christ Jesus." Some translations say, "Pray without ceasing." I know it's hard to give thanks and to keep on praying when things don't seem to be going the way we want them to. But we never know what is truly happening behind the gates of heaven when we pray. "Since ancient times no one has heard, no ear has perceived, no eye has seen any God besides you, who acts on behalf of those who wait for him" (Isa. 64:4). *Since ancient times.*

Before we were even born, before our children were born, God was busy acting on behalf of his beloved children, and we can be assured that he still is today. "Jesus Christ is the same yesterday and today and forever" (Heb. 13:8). We can hardly comprehend this in a world where literally everything changes. We don't always know the way he will answer us, but we are assured in Psalm 17:6 that he will: "I call on you, my God, for you will answer me; turn your ear to me and hear my prayer."

Hang on to all these promises when you are praying for the same things over and over. In Abbey's diagnosis, little has changed during the last eight years. However, I could never have imagined how far she'd come. My sweet baby, whose eyes hadn't yet lit up at three months, now lights up every room she enters. There is only One who knows how my prayers were really answered, and I can't wait to hear all about it.

Father in heaven, you alone are capable of hearing my petitions and coming to my child's aid. Your Word promises me that you answer. I may not know how you are answering my prayers, and I may not understand those answers in this life, but I will keep on praying with a heart of thanksgiving, because I know you hear me. Thank you, Lord. In Jesus's name, amen.

DIGGING DEEPER

1. What are the prayer requests for your child that are still unanswered?
2. What are some prayers that *have* been answered over the last few years?
3. What does Isaiah 59:1 tell you about who God is?

WHEN WE CAN'T FIX IT

Jocelyn

Therefore, holy brothers and sisters, who share in the
heavenly calling, fix your thoughts on Jesus, whom
we acknowledge as our apostle and high priest.

HEBREWS 3:1

Like most dads, Rob Wurzel likes to fix things that are broken. But the one thing he wants to fix more than anything else—his daughter's brain damage—he can't.

"I wrestled a really long time with trying to figure out why God allowed Reagan's metabolic crisis to happen, and I believe most people probably have that hang up with God," said Rob. "But I learned that God isn't always in the business of letting us know what his plans are, and it is probably for the best because we wouldn't want to go down that path if we knew how hard things would be. However, no matter how tough or how broken everything seems, he can use that to make himself known and further his kingdom. That is what I see happening in our story."

In Rob's experience, if he dwells on trying to figure out the logic and the reasons behind all that his family has been through, he gets stuck. "When I do that, I'm going to be paralyzed in moving forward because

I'm only going to be looking back. And there is no way I can fix any of this. The only thing that has worked that I can do is pray and rely on God, and that is how I am continuing to move forward each day. Each day has [its] own set of problems, and each day I know God will give me the strength and help me get through it."

As parents, we want to fix whatever is wrong for our children, and it hurts when we can't. We must take these frustrations to our heavenly Father, the only one who can redeem our hardships.

Still, according to Scripture, we do have some "fixing" of our own to do:

1. *We must* fix *God's Word on our hearts.* "Fix these words of mine in your hearts and minds; tie them as symbols on your hands and bind them on your foreheads. Teach them to your children, talking about them when you sit at home and when you walk along the road, when you lie down and when you get up" (Deut. 11:18–19). No matter where we are, or what time of day it is, God's Word is to be paramount in our lives—and in our children's.

2. *We must* fix *our thoughts on Jesus.* "Therefore, holy brothers and sisters, who share in the heavenly calling, fix your thoughts on Jesus, whom we acknowledge as our apostle and high priest" (Heb. 3:1). If we back up to the last few verses of Hebrews chapter 2, we read the reason we are to fix our thoughts on Jesus: He is merciful and faithful (v. 17), and "because he himself suffered when he was tempted, he is able to help those who are being tempted" (v. 18). When we are tempted to despair or to doubt, he can help us.

3. *We must* fix *our eyes on Jesus.* "Let us run with perseverance the race marked out for us, fixing our eyes on Jesus, the pioneer and perfecter of faith. For the joy set before him he endured the cross, scorning its shame, and sat down at the right hand of the

throne of God. Consider him who endured such opposition from sinners, so that you will not grow weary and lose heart" (Heb. 12:1–3). Fixing our eyes on Jesus, rather than on our race, is the way to keep from losing heart. The hardships won't disappear, but he'll keep us from growing so weary that we quit this path he's marked out for us.

Most of us, like Rob, want to fix the things that are broken. When we can't, let's remember what we can fix: God's Word in our hearts, and our thoughts and eyes on Jesus.

Dear Lord, you know my heart aches when I can't make things better for my child. I surrender these things to you, and leave them in your capable hands. Please help me fix your Word in my heart and help me focus my thoughts and eyes on you. In Jesus's name, amen.

DIGGING DEEPER

1. What do you most want to "fix" right now?
2. What have you done toward that goal? Have you surrendered the outcome to God?
3. How can you fix God's Word in your heart, and your thoughts and eyes on him, a little more?

THREE

Pulling Weeds
Digging Out That Which Entangles

Therefore do not let sin reign in your mortal body
so that you obey its evil desires.
ROMANS 6:12

DO YOU LOVE ME?

Kimberly

For I am convinced that neither death nor life,
neither angels nor demons, neither the present nor the
future, nor any powers, neither height nor depth, nor
anything else in all creation, will be able to separate us
from the love of God that is in Christ Jesus our Lord.

ROMANS 8:38-39

One of the most difficult things about losing a child, or having a child with a disability, is wrestling with the questions. I often find myself asking, "Does God love me? Does he *really* love me?" Sometimes in quiet solitude, I start to think that maybe I'm insignificant to God, that he forgot to look out for me, that I'm not a "good enough" Christian to deserve his favor and blessing, or that maybe he just doesn't love me the way I long to be loved.

Though wrestling with these thoughts is normal, not one of them is true. In fact, Jeremiah 31:3 says, "The LORD appeared to us in the past, saying: 'I have loved you with an everlasting love; I have drawn you with unfailing kindness.'" You can feel the tenderness of God's heart in the way he spoke these words to assure us that his love for us will never end.

It's hard to grasp the depth of the love of Christ. The depth of love required to live a sinless life only to die a sinner's death is unfathomable. Can we wrap our mind around what it meant to pay a sinner's price before a holy God the Father? Sometimes we are so focused on ourselves that we forget that the gospel of Christ was carved out in flesh and blood. He lived. He loved. He died a gruesome death that belonged to you and to me. He took on the weight of God's wrath, something we cannot begin to comprehend, for our sake. Why? "For God so *loved* the world that he gave his one and only Son, that whoever believes in him shall not perish but have eternal life" (John 3:16, emphasis added). The gates of heaven opened, and Christ came to lavish his love on a broken world by giving them the hope of eternity.

When I find myself overwhelmed by the weight of my loss, and the responsibility of my calling to care for Abbey, I have a hard time remembering that God does love me. I have to try to take my heart, soul, and mind to a place that connects with the seriousness of my need for a Savior and the encouragement that comes from his act of love for me on the cross. When I face myself squarely in the mirror and see the sinner I am, the wretchedness of my heart apart from God, I am quickly brought to my knees in humility.

God loves us. I shouldn't have to remind myself of how much he loves me, but I do. I do because my situation taxes me physically, emotionally, and spiritually. It's the honesty of my heart that draws me closer to him. So it's OK to cry out and ask the Lord, "Do you love me God?" Weep at his feet, and then beg him to give you the strength it will take to seek him out in the Word, and find out what he has to say about his love for you. Cling to the words of Romans 8:38–39: "For I am convinced that neither death nor life, neither angels nor demons, neither the present nor the future, nor any powers, neither height nor depth, nor anything else in all creation, will be able to separate us from the love of God that is in Christ Jesus our Lord."

Lord, I'm hurting today and I need to feel your love for me. Help me, Father, to know and grasp your everlasting love. To remember that it has no conditions or boundaries and that nothing can separate me from your love. In Jesus's name, amen.

DIGGING DEEPER

1. Describe your relationship with Christ and your understanding of his great love for you.
2. What lies have you believed that distort your image of the God who loves you?
3. What Scriptures can you find that disprove these lies?

GOOD-BYE, GUILT!

Jocelyn

In Him we have redemption through His blood,
the forgiveness of our trespasses, according to the
riches of His grace which He lavished on us.

EPHESIANS 1:7-8 (NASB)

Six months after Laura and Craig Slezak's daughter was diagnosed with Angelman syndrome, Laura confessed on her blog, "I feel like I am failing at a lot of things: getting Ava enough therapy, remembering to pay bills, finding time to play with my kids, remembering to close the garage door, responding to important emails and texts, eating food, whatever. This is something I've got to get free from."[1]

Sound familiar? No matter what your child's special need is, chances are you've experienced guilt—reasonable or not—over some aspect of your journey. Gillian Marchenko sometimes deems the beginning of her daughter's life as Gillian's "saddest failure" in terms of her faith, and ability to cope and love.[2] Brian Riley battles "almost never-ending guilt" for not being able to engage enough with his nonverbal son or with his other two children.[3]

Three of Priscilla Rhoades's children were diagnosed with autism at the same time. "I was upset a lot, both before and after the diagnosis, thinking maybe some past sin of mine had caused what happened to my children. It wasn't until the Lord showed me the story of the man born blind in John 9 that I was set free from those thoughts. Even now, when they try to return, I use his Word to combat them."

Whether we're haunted by our initial reactions to our children's disabilities or needled by whispers that we could be doing better for our kids, guilt can become an all-too-familiar companion if we let it.

There is a big difference between the prick of conscience after lashing out in anger and the barbs of false guilt over human limitations or circumstances beyond our control. The former is the Holy Spirit prodding us toward repentance; the latter is Satan flinging discouragement and shame at us for any reason that might stick. Logic need not apply.

While the Holy Spirit transforms us by renewing our minds so we can do God's will (Rom. 12:2), Satan, the Deceiver, wants to destroy us. How clever of him to masquerade as our conscience! And how utterly destructive if we allow him to shackle us to false guilt.

Friends, it's time to give guilt an eviction notice. God knows your limitations. He made you human, and does not expect you to be all-knowing, all-wise, omnipresent, or omnipotent. If it's false guilt that's squeezing your heart, kick it to the curb. If you've done wrong, ask God's forgiveness, receive it, and move on. God forgives you. It's time to forgive yourself.

What does that mean, exactly? It means we ask for God's forgiveness, and we believe and accept that he is faithful and just to purify us (1 John 1:9). We allow his grace to cover all our mistakes and missed chances, because his grace is sufficient (2 Cor. 12:9). We see ourselves as God sees us: washed white as snow.

Remember, grace comes with no strings attached (or else it would not be grace at all). It's the gift that saves us (Eph. 2:8–9) and sustains us throughout this life. John said, "Of [Jesus's] fullness we have all received, and grace upon grace" (John 1:16 NASB). *Grace upon grace.* Accept that glorious gift, and banish guilt—true or false—from your heart.

Lord, forgive me for my wrongs, and cover my shortcomings with your grace. Make something beautiful from this mess. Help me say good-bye to guilt and live in your fullness instead. In Jesus's name, amen.

DIGGING DEEPER
1. In what areas of your life do you struggle with guilt?
2. When you accept God's grace in those areas, how does that change your perspective?
3. What do you need to forgive yourself for today?

THE REINS OF SIN

Kimberly

Therefore, since we are surrounded by such a great cloud
of witnesses, let us throw off everything that hinders
and the sin that so easily entangles. And let us run with
perseverance the race marked out for us, fixing our eyes
on Jesus, the pioneer and perfecter of faith. For the
joy set before him he endured the cross, scorning its
shame, and sat down at the right hand of the throne of
God. Consider him who endured such opposition from
sinners, so that you will not grow weary and lose heart.

HEBREWS 12:1-3

Monday nights we take Abbey to an amazing facility that offers equine therapy for disabled children and adults. When she's there, she is in one of her favorite places on earth. Her instructor, Kathy, has been with her since the first lesson. We still laugh about how she kicked and screamed and didn't want to get on the horse. It has been four years since Kathy first lugged Abbey up onto a saddle. She has made great strides since then and continues to surprise us with how much she is capable of. However, she tends to throw the reins down to be funny, and on a horse, this is not just a bad habit; it's a very dangerous one.

Kathy has been working hard to get Abbey to stop this behavior. She never gives up on her. They stop the horse, have a talk, and start again. They do this over and over if they must. The goal is to keep Abbey safe and grow her into a more mature rider.

How many of us are just like Abbey with those reins? We have habits and hang-ups that could be passed off as just "bad." We might even think they're funny. But they are really so dangerous. Hebrews 12 says sin entangles us. James 1:15 warns us of the consequences of sin: "Then, after desire has conceived, it gives birth to sin; and sin, when it is full-grown, gives birth to death." Death is no laughing matter.

Our heavenly Father wants to keep us safe and grow us into mature believers. Colossians chapter 2 gives us some guidelines for spiritual fullness in Christ. Among them, in verse 14, Paul reminds us that our sin left us indebted to God the Creator; it stood against us and condemned us. But Christ came and "has taken it away, nailing it to the cross."

Should we lose heart or be overwhelmed by sin, we need only look to Christ, who overcame it. In fact, 1 Corinthians 10:13 promises, "No temptation has overtaken you except what is common to mankind. And God is faithful; he will not let you be tempted beyond what you can bear. But when you are tempted, he will also provide a way out so that you can endure it."

Overcoming sin and living in spiritual fullness with Christ requires a tight hold on his Word and on Christ himself. We can't just coast through life's lessons and drop the reins whenever we feel like it. Christ has so much more in store for us if we hold tight, learn from the best Instructor, and keep walking. Hebrews 12:3 reminds us to "consider him who endured such opposition from sinners, so that you will not grow weary and lose heart."

Lord, help me. Help me not to make light of habits that keep me from enjoying the ride we're on together. Help me to hold on to you and be safe in your care. Help me not to let go of you or buy into the lie that sin isn't that big of a deal, especially in a world that thinks sin is funny. Thank you for stopping me in my tracks, for having a talk with me, and for letting me start over again. In Jesus's name, amen.

DIGGING DEEPER

1. What sin have you been making light of in your life?
2. How has God provided a way out of this temptation for you?
3. In what ways can you look to him to help you not grow weary in the fight against sin?

SAYING NO TO IDOLATRY

Jocelyn

Therefore, my dear friends, flee from idolatry.
1 CORINTHIANS 10:14

What comes to mind when you think of an idol? A small carved image? The golden calf formed by the Israelites while Moses was busy convening with God on the mountain? The life-size bronze statue in the lobby of your favorite Chinese restaurant? Perhaps a more postmodern form of idolatry comes to mind. We Americans know how to worship athletes, movie stars, and the almighty dollar, don't we?

An idol is anything to which we assign the utmost devotion, even above God himself. We Christians are fairly good at identifying when pursuits of success, fame, and money cross the line into sinful idolatry. But surely devotion to our children with special needs doesn't apply? After all, Philippians 2:3–4 reads, "In humility value others above yourselves, not looking to your own interests but each of you to the interests of the others." How can caring for our kids be anything but sacrificial service?

Simple, says Gloria Williams: when it takes the place of honoring God. Gloria, a mother of four adopted children, discovered idolatry in her own home and heart. It was her kids—or rather, keeping them happy.

Placing our children's interests above our own is humility; placing their interests above God's interests—that's idolatry. For Gloria, it didn't happen all at once. Two of her children had special needs. One daughter has reactive attachment disorder, making it difficult for her to bond with others and display common courtesies. Her son Monroe was born addicted to crack and he struggled with a number of medical and psychiatric complications. Parenting these children certainly required sacrifices and concessions. Monroe's medications lowered his metabolism and increased his appetite. He was smart, funny, and loved by all who knew him. Most of the time, he was a wonderful companion. But in those rare instances when he became angry, he was so large he couldn't be managed, and the police had to be called to restrain him. "We had to do things a certain way to keep one or the other from getting upset," Gloria said.

But when Gloria noticed her special children's needs were ruling the home, including preventing the family from attending church, Gloria asked herself, "Who am I serving in this moment? Is it my daughter? My son? The situation? Or is it the Lord? What does the Lord want me to do?"

After Monroe passed away suddenly at the age of sixteen, Gloria's struggle with setting boundaries with her kids intensified—and she didn't have the strength to fight it. "I wondered, *Is this the last thing they ask for and then they'll be gone?* So I got them what they wanted, I was more lax with rules, and then, even with school. I just kept thinking, *Will this be my last fight with them?* But I can't ruin them because I think they might die. I had to get over the fear of losing the next child. My decisions were hurting the kids. I had to get back on it, with helping my kids to be who they needed to be in the Lord."

Two years after her son's passing, Gloria realized what had happened. "I was abandoning the Lord and his principles. It was subtle. It looks so good and it looks right, but it's wrong. Finally, I turned it around. Not letting your special-needs child become an idol before the Lord is huge."

Abandoning the Lord's standards for honesty, integrity, modesty, etc., is never in our children's best interests. When we keep God in his rightful place as Lord over all, the entire family benefits.

God, you are the Lord and there is no other. Help me live this out by placing you above all else, including my children. Show me when I approach the line between biblically serving my children and allowing their needs to drive a wedge between us and you. In Jesus's name, amen.

DIGGING DEEPER

1. How do you deny your own interests when serving your child?
2. What aspect of your life may be in danger of becoming more important than serving God?
3. What is one thing you can do this week to "flee from idolatry"?

WHEN CHURCHES HURT

Kimberly

And let us consider how we may spur one another on toward
love and good deeds, not giving up meeting together,
as some are in the habit of doing, but encouraging one
another—and all the more as you see the Day approaching.

HEBREWS 10:24-25

When Abbey was diagnosed with cerebral palsy, my church watched me spiral into serious depression and marriage difficulty. Elders "noticed" I was not attending church regularly, yet they never bothered to call me to see how I was doing. Meanwhile, I battled suicidal thoughts and crippling sadness. When I shared some of my emotional struggle with a church leader as I asked his counsel for our finances, he told me to "get up off the couch, and make up your mind that you are going to go to work." Ultimately, my church asked my husband to leave his job as youth pastor so we could heal and find a better church fit. Instead of helping us heal, our church only deepened our wounds.

Anne-Marie Wurzel felt abandoned by her church when her daughter suffered a metabolic crisis causing severe brain damage. "Only one of the campus ministers visited in the hospital to pray for us, and no one came to pray over Reagan once we were home," she said. "When I told a friend who worked in the children's ministry that there's just no place for us and that they should try to do a special-needs program, the response was, 'We thought about it and just couldn't figure out how to make it work.' Meanwhile they send teams to Africa multiple times a year." More than a year and a half passed before the Wurzels found a church with a special-needs program. "That's 547 days and a lot of Sundays longing for a place our entire family could go," she wrote.[4]

Some of you may wonder if it's worth the trouble of finding a church at all. But let's take a look at what Jesus says about his bride, the church. In Acts 20:28, Paul gives this charge to the elders of the church of Ephesus: "Keep watch over yourselves and all the flock of which the Holy Spirit has made you overseers. Be shepherds of the church of God, which he bought with his own blood." In Ephesians 5:25–27, Paul wrote, "Husbands, love your wives, just as Christ loved the church and gave himself up for her to make her holy, cleansing her by the washing with water through the word, and to present her to himself as a radiant church, without stain or wrinkle or any other blemish, but holy and blameless." Jesus not only deeply loves the church, but he gave up his life for her. If I don't feel the same way about God's people—even though I've been hurt and disappointed by many of them—then I don't have the heart of Christ.

The Bible is full of stories of broken and messy churches. We are all broken and messy people. But to love the church like Christ does, we have to commit to both forgiveness and fellowship. After a two-year break from ministry, my husband and I returned to youth ministry at the church he grew up in. And while it hasn't been perfect and has even been painful at times, God is giving me a heart for his people again. With time, he has even helped me forgive and love the church that hurt us.

Friends, let's not let our past dictate our future involvement with the body of Christ. It might mean changing churches or helping to change the church you already have (see "Resources" at the back of this book to help with this). But let us not give up on meeting together and encouraging one another. Let's ask the Lord to continue to heal us and give us his heart for his people.

Lord, give me your heart for the church. You love the church, and died for it. Your Word says that nothing, not even hades, will prevail against it. Help me to look at your people with the same heart of love and compassion that you do. In Jesus's name, amen.

DIGGING DEEPER

1. In what ways do you share the heart of Christ for his church?
2. In what areas do you need God's forgiveness and healing in regard to your relationship with your local church?
3. What steps can you take to move forward in faith by reengaging with a church? Can you return to the church you attended? Or find a new one in which to heal—one that supports your child's unique needs?

SELF-SABOTAGE

Jocelyn

I know that good itself does not dwell in me, that is,
in my sinful nature. For I have the desire to do what is
good, but I cannot carry it out. For I do not do the good I
want to do, but the evil I do not want to do—this I keep
on doing. Now if I do what I do not want to do, it is no
longer I who do it, but it is sin living in me that does it.

ROMANS 7:18-20

Polly Marchenko, who was born with Down syndrome, was two and a half years old when her physical therapist assigned her three hours a day to be strapped into a wooden stander. The goal was to help her build muscle mass to make standing and walking possible later on.

It didn't take long, however, for Polly to fight it. "This is where the sabotage emerged," wrote her mother, Gillian. "She figured out how to hike her little rear up over the thick leather strap that circled her middle, thus creating a ledge to sit on while she was supposed to be standing. She pulled the Velcro strap apart one handed, attempting to free herself. Eventually, it was all out war. Polly kicked the stander, pulled off the strap, and tried to push over the large wooden base."[5] After a while, Polly gave up her antics, did her time, and grew stronger as a result.

If we're honest with ourselves, there are many times when we are just like Polly, shoving and kicking at that which would make us stronger. Maybe you can relate to Anne-Marie Wurzel, who shared, "Some days I neglect God (recently, it's a lot of days). I don't want to, but it happens. I wake up like I was shot out of a cannon to cries from across the house. *SHE'S UP!* Get her meds, change her g-tube site, get the formula ready, get her food ready, weigh it, pray she eats it, try to give her formula by mouth, hope she cooperates, *where's the coffee?!*"[6]

At the end of many long days, all the Bravo TV shows stacked up on her DVR prove too tempting to ignore. For others of us, we choose Facebook instead of the Good Book; we choose Pinterest over prayer. But when we push God aside or give him the scraps of our time and energy, we sabotage ourselves. As Anne-Marie said, we don't want to, but it happens.

It happens to the best of us, in fact. In Romans 7:18–20, Paul confesses, "I have the desire to do what is good, but I cannot carry it out. For I do not do the good I want to do, but the evil I do not want to do—this I keep on doing. Now if I do what I do not want to do, it is no longer I who do it, but it is sin living in me that does it."

No one is immune to good intentions gone awry. If sin is the sickness that sabotages our path to healing and wholeness, then what is the cure?

Jesus. But here's the hard part—we're going to have to spend time with him and in the Word if we want to build our spiritual muscle mass, even if we don't feel like it. "Remain in me, as I also remain in you. No branch can bear fruit by itself; it must remain in the vine. Neither can you bear fruit unless you remain in me" (John 15:4).

It may feel easier to scroll through the phone, or unwind in front of Netflix, or clean out the junk drawer, or unsubscribe from every junk email list in our in-box. But if we use these things as distractions from our spiritual condition, as crutches for our injured souls, they won't hold our weight. Only when we abide in Christ and take advantage of our own "standers"—healthy community, Bible reading (or listening), worship, prayer—will we grow stronger and bear fruit. It takes discipline. But this is one therapy that's guaranteed to work.

Lord, I confess that I sometimes sabotage my own ability to live this life well. Help me catch myself before I do so. Help me turn to you as my default mode. Teach me what it means to abide in Christ. In Jesus's name, amen.

DIGGING DEEPER
1. Which spiritual "stander" do you kick against the most?
2. How do you tend to sabotage yourself?
3. Name one thing you can do today to dwell more closely with Christ.

SIBLING RIVALRY

Kimberly

A friend loves at all times, and a brother
is born for a time of adversity.

PROVERBS 17:17

Barb Dittrich's daughter struggled with her brother's hemophilia diagnosis. "I did everything the experts recommended for kids like her who have siblings with a diagnosis," Barb wrote. "I spent intentional time making special outings alone with her. I listened and validated her feelings. I never shamed her. I also established regular Sib-Shops in our area, so that she could connect to other peers who understood her frustration. Even so, it felt like the animosity she had for her brother would never end."[7]

My husband and I have seen the same thing in our house with our disabled daughter. Abbey has a tantrum if I try to spend quality time with our oldest son while she is within eyesight. She will scream, fall to the ground, or even lash out at him if she can reach him. Her insecurities have been difficult to experience and watch. This kind of insecurity holds hands with jealousy and envy.

We can all relate to this on some level, can't we? When we misplace our security in things that can be taken away—jobs, material

possessions, beauty, health, talents, money, expectations, dreams—we
are vulnerable. We're left feeling shaken when we lose what we relied
on to bring us comfort and confidence. But when we know to whom we
belong, who holds our lives in *his* hands, we are secure indeed. After the
Lord delivered David from Saul, David said, "The LORD is my rock, my
fortress and my deliverer; my God is my rock, in whom I take refuge,
my shield and the horn of my salvation. He is my stronghold, my refuge and my savior—from violent people you save me" (2 Sam. 22:2–3).
We too can have the confidence to call God our rock and our salvation.

Security in Christ also keeps us from making poor decisions and
damaging relationships. We have had to help Jayden get past Abbey's
outbursts and tantrums and help him understand her disabilities so
that it doesn't put a wedge between them. We have had to discipline
Abbey for her reactions to her jealousy. Behind her jealousy, insecurity
tells Abbey I love Jayden more than her, but security doesn't compare
our love at all.

How often has insecurity, jealousy, or envy broken down the trust
in relationships with the people we love? Paul rebuked the Corinthian
church for its jealousy. "You are still worldly. For since there is jealousy
and quarreling among you, are you not worldly? Are you not acting like
mere humans?" (1 Cor. 3:3). James 4:1 tells us these quarrels come from
desires that battle within us.

Instead of this, security in Christ looks to God and trusts that he
is enough for us because of his character. "I will proclaim the name
of the LORD. Oh, praise the greatness of our God! He is the Rock, his
works are perfect, and all his ways are just. A faithful God who does no
wrong, upright and just is he" (Deut. 32:3–4).

As secure as Abbey could feel in me, a flawed and sinful parent, how
much more secure should we be in God? There is no room for the pain
of insecurity in the arms of our perfect, faithful, and just Father.

As our children grow, Jayden is becoming a kind and compassionate advocate for his sister despite her tantrums. Barb Dittrich shared,

"Adversity, as it turns out, has made my children closer . . . MUCH closer."[8] With our security in the character and love of Christ, we too can overcome the jealousies that plague our relationships and distract us from our walk with Christ.

> *Dear Lord, you are a perfect parent, and my children are yours. I pray that you would remove any insecurity or jealousy from our home and our lives. Forgive me for the ways this has shown itself in my own life, and help me to find my security in you alone. In Jesus's name, amen.*

DIGGING DEEPER

1. Is there any area of your life where you are struggling with insecurity?
2. What are the deeper fears behind that insecurity that need to be dealt with?
3. In what ways can you turn to God to find true peace and contentment?

MIND GAMES

Jocelyn

We demolish arguments and every pretension that sets
itself up against the knowledge of God, and we take
captive every thought to make it obedient to Christ.
2 CORINTHIANS 10:5

It happened before. It could happen again. The thought flashes through
Anne-Marie Wurzel's mind quicker than she can wipe her daughter's nose with a trembling hand. For two-and-a-half-year-old Reagan, there's no such thing as a "common" cold. Because of her rare genetic disorder (GA-1), any illness could induce a metabolic crisis that causes brain damage. When it happened at the age of thirteen months, doctors told Anne-Marie and her husband, Rob, that Reagan would never walk, talk, smile, laugh, or go to school. Reagan does smile and laugh, and she even walks in a walker now. But the thought of losing those milestones all over again is haunting.

"When Reagan isn't feeling well, Rob and I are on pins and needles, while texting her geneticist about the day's developments and wondering if this is serious enough to go to the hospital. . . . It takes a ridiculous mental toll," she shared. "It's like the Devil is playing mind games with me."[9]

Satan loves to play mind games with each of us. Whatever our vulnerability, whether it's fear, anger, resentment, or self-reliance, he will prey on it. Our very thoughts are a spiritual battleground. "Put on the full armor of God, so that you can take your stand against the devil's schemes. For our struggle is not against flesh and blood, but against the rulers, against the authorities, against the powers of this dark world and against the spiritual forces of evil in the heavenly realms" (Eph. 6:11–12).

Paul goes on to describe the armor we must wear. Truth is both our protection and our weapon (vv. 14, 17) as we take captive every thought and make it obedient to Christ (2 Cor. 10:5), and we find treasures of truth in Scripture.

When Anne-Marie feels like life is out of control, she reminds herself that God is in control. "In his hand is the life of every creature and the breath of all mankind" (Job 12:10). When we find ourselves crippled by fear: "They will have no fear of bad news; their hearts are steadfast, trusting in the LORD" (Ps. 112:7). When we think we can't keep going: "I can do all this through him who gives me strength" (Phil. 4:13). When we harbor bitterness and resentment against those who have hurt us: "[Love] does not dishonor others, it is not self-seeking, it is not easily angered, it keeps no record of wrongs" (1 Cor. 13:5).

For the Wurzels, the possibilities of more illness once Reagan is in school are terrifying. When Reagan suffered her first metabolic crisis after being discharged from the hospital, "We were just heading into the darkest deepest forest you could imagine," said Anne-Marie. "I don't want to go back there. I just have to trust God and trust that his plan is way bigger and provides him more glory than what my plan might be [Prov. 3:5]."

Whatever thought is beginning to sprout in your mind, if it doesn't match what the Bible says, take it captive. Dig it out before it takes root. Replace it with the truths in God's Word, and claim victory one thought at a time.

Lord, help me be alert and of sober mind (1 Peter 5:8). Help me detect thoughts and feelings that are not of you and combat them with the truths found in your Word. Give me clarity and strength for the battle of the mind, as I make every thought obedient to Christ. In Jesus's name, amen.

DIGGING DEEPER

1. Which recurring thought do you have that you know is not grounded in truth?
2. What does the Bible say about that notion?
3. What is one verse you'd like to memorize or post on your fridge?

CONFRONTING MY FRIENDS—AND MYSELF

Kimberly

Why do you look at the speck of sawdust
in your brother's eye and pay no attention to the plank
in your own eye? How can you say to your brother, "Let
me take the speck out of your eye," when all the time
there is a plank in your own eye? You hypocrite, first
take the plank out of your own eye, and then you will
see clearly to remove the speck from your brother's eye.

MATTHEW 7:3-5

One second I was smiling as my friend told me about her daughter's ice-skating party, and the next moment, it occurred to me that our girls are in the same grade, and had Abbey not been disabled, she'd probably be skating right along. I'm not sure at what point my grief and sadness turned to anger, but below the surface of my smile and almost four years of friendship, my heart is still broken that it didn't occur to my friend to invite Abbey along. Since then, my friend and I have cried through these issues together. It was an opportunity for both of us to learn to truly love and forgive each other like Christ.

Abbey is fourteen years old now and has a Sunday school class full of girls her age. I have lots of friends outside of church with daughters who are also Abbey's age. We do not experience the same things with our girls, but that doesn't mean we can't *do life* together.

I wonder sometimes what my role is supposed to be in making this happen. I've cried over feeling forgotten or left out on so many occasions that I can barely type through my tears. I haven't invited my friends' little girls over to play. It's a delicate situation when your child is disabled, because you don't want to force friendship on anyone. Children aren't comfortable with Abbey's drool and diapers or her social interactions, and I've never felt it was fair to ask a child to be her friend if he or she didn't want to. But maybe children just need to be taught how? It hurts that other parents haven't done this with their children.

When we are hurt or angry with a family member or friend, before we launch off on a confrontation, let's first take a deeper look at ourselves and examine our own hearts. Matthew 7 implores us to do so. Ephesians 4:25–27 warns us, "Each of you must put off falsehood and speak truthfully to your neighbor, for we are all members of one body. 'In your anger do not sin': Do not let the sun go down while you are still angry, and do not give the devil a foothold."

In my Bible, chapter four of Ephesians is titled "Unity and Maturity in the Body of Christ." As I study this, I'm challenged that the chapter ends with this: "Be kind and compassionate to one another, forgiving each other, just as in Christ God forgave you" (v. 32). We are all going to fail miserably at times, but with these guidelines for how to handle ourselves, we can make this painful and difficult journey a little easier. There will always be grief when our friends' children are growing and thriving and experiencing life while ours are growing and *surviving* and experiencing a different kind of life. But God can turn the process of working through that grief with our friends into something beautiful. It's what he does.

> *Lord, help me examine my own heart before you. Search me and know me, and see if there is any offensive way in me. Help me*

*be a better friend by communicating my needs and being honest
about my hurts before they can become a foothold or a bitter root.
In Jesus's name, amen.*

Digging Deeper

1. When you examine your own heart, what offensive ways do you
   see?
2. Are there hurts that you need to deal with in any of your
   relationships?
3. How can you better communicate your needs to your close
   friends and family?

I LOVE HORSES MORE THAN YOU

Kimberly

Where your treasure is, there your heart will be also.
MATTHEW 6:21

Despite the fact that Abbey is a nonverbal child, she can still get her point across. One night at dinner she started to throw a *massive* temper tantrum because Ryan, instead of me, was going to feed her dinner. When it was obvious she wasn't going to stop, Ryan took her to her room for a time-out and to calm her down. After really going at it with her for a while in her room, Ryan had to leave. Pausing at the doorway of her room, he told her he had to go and signed "I love you" to her. This got her angry again, so she leaned toward him and signed back, "I love horses!" Now Ryan and I were both cracking up! She wasn't sure how *not* to say "I love you" back, so she settled for telling him she loved horses more. How about that for a preteen response to a dad she's mad at? It was hilarious.

Aren't we just like that when God wants us to do something we don't want to do? How about when he wants us to *stop* doing something we shouldn't be doing? Don't we just sort of throw an adult temper tantrum at God and, in effect, sign back, "I love _____ more than you!" Only this isn't funny. The truth is, sometimes we love socializing more than hearing God's Word at church. Sometimes we love reading a good book more than reading God's Word. Sometimes we love sin more than doing what God's Word says to do. We probably wouldn't literally collapse to the ground and kick and scream, but we can ignore God altogether and pretend we don't know the truth. There are about a million ways to get our point across to God without ever saying a single word. But he knows our hearts. He knows our signs.

Riding horses is a great thing for Abbey. I want Abbey to love horses. I even love that she loves them. But they should never take the place of her father who adores her, knows what's best for her, and sometimes disciplines her out of his love. Jesus tells us of the place God should take in our lives in Matthew 22:37–38: "Jesus replied: '"Love the Lord your God with all your heart and with all your soul and with all your mind." This is the first and greatest commandment.'"

We know that even a good thing can become an idol and pull us away from worshipping and loving God this way. First Corinthians 10:14 is clear: "Therefore, my dear friends, flee from idolatry." We have to put things in their proper place. Only one thing or person can occupy the throne of our hearts.

Horses can be very dangerous. There is a reason you have to find the correct temperament of horse to put a disabled child on. They're huge, they're heavy, and with one swift kick to the wrong place they can kill a person. Sometimes the things we love can also be extremely dangerous if we do not take caution and do them the way God wants them to be done. First Corinthians 10:12 warns us, "If you think you are standing firm, be careful that you don't fall!" We must be careful that we aren't finding ourselves a slave to sin, which leads to death (Rom. 6:16).

Abbey cannot fathom how much her daddy loves her. Turn to Romans 5:6–8 for a reminder of how lavishly our Father loves us. When we are the recipient of that kind of lavish love, we are compelled to respond and, out of our own great love for him, do our best to know him who died for us and follow him in obedience. He created the world to be enjoyed, to be lived in, to be a part of—but not to worship.

> *Dear Lord, thank you for loving me the way that you do. Forgive me for loving the things of this world more than you. Help me to put things and people in their proper place in my life. In Jesus's name, amen.*

DIGGING DEEPER

1. What are you loving more than God right now?
2. Are you throwing an internal adult temper tantrum at God because you don't like what his Word has to say? If so, what about?
3. What steps can you take to restore your love relationship with him?

FOUR

Parched
When Hope Withers

You, God, are my God,
earnestly I seek you;
I thirst for you,
my whole being longs for you,
in a dry and parched land
where there is no water.

PSALM 63:1

WAITING OUT THE STORM

Kimberly

Whoever dwells in the shelter of the Most High
will rest in the shadow of the Almighty.

PSALM 91:1

E very ounce of emotion I had crashed down on me like a torrential
rain. Grief pounded relentlessly on the roof of my soul, threatening
to bring my entire house down. The winds of *Why?*, of change, and of
disappointment raged together in a perfect storm. I had lost a son, bur-
ied a dream, and walked away from a graveside instead of a maternity
ward. I left with empty arms instead of open ones. Even several months
later, it felt like only yesterday.

In times like this, where do we go to find a shelter? Where is the
Rock we can lean on? What are the promises God has for us when it
seems that the floods will overtake us?

Like David in Psalm 69:1, I cried out, "Save me, O God, for the
waters have come up to my neck."

I wrestled with my emotions and tried to sort out my faith all at the
same time. What good are my emotions if they are not seen through the
lens of my beliefs? If there is no reconciliation of the two, then I am in a
state of utter confusion. The Spirit inside of me wants me to know, see,

feel, and experience God through this . . . and my flesh wants to shake its fist in anger at the sky and walk away from it all. They are at war, the flesh and Spirit. Paul talked about this in Romans 7:21–25: "So I find this law at work: Although I want to do good, evil is right there with me. For in my inner being I delight in God's law; but I see another law at work in me, waging war against the law of my mind and making me a prisoner of the law of sin at work within me. What a wretched man I am! Who will rescue me from this body that is subject to death? Thanks be to God, who delivers me through Jesus Christ our Lord!"

Through Christ, we are assured that we can overcome the flesh. His Spirit will win, because the power of Christ who conquered the grave is also at work in us. Second Corinthians 12:9 declares, "He said to me, 'My grace is sufficient for you, for my power is made perfect in weakness.' Therefore I will boast all the more gladly about my weaknesses, so that Christ's power may rest on me."

Isaiah 43:1–3 emphasizes that God will carry us through this by saying, "This is what the LORD says—he who created you, Jacob, he who formed you, Israel: 'Do not fear, for I have redeemed you; I have summoned you by name; you are mine. When you pass through the waters, I will be with you; and when you pass through the rivers, they will not sweep over you. When you walk through the fire, you will not be burned; the flames will not set you ablaze. For I am the LORD your God, the Holy One of Israel, your Savior.'" Oh, how I need these promises!

Dear friend, if you find yourself waiting out a storm of your own, do so under the shelter of his wings. "Whoever dwells in the shelter of the Most High will rest in the shadow of the Almighty" (Ps. 91:1).

Three months after the death of my son, I wrote in my journal, "I do believe that eventually the winds and seas of my soul will calm, because they obey the voice of their Creator and Master. When they do, having rested under his shelter, I'll step out and feel the sun on my face again." Though I still miss my son and always will, I do indeed feel the sun— and the Son—again.

Lord, you know the storm I'm in. You are the shelter I run to in my time of need. You are a Mighty God and the only one with the power to save me. Thank you for never giving up on me as I sort this out with you, and for being my refuge. In Jesus's name, amen.

DIGGING DEEPER

1. What storm is threatening you today?
2. Where are you finding shelter from today's storm—in the Most High God, or somewhere else?
3. What is one thing you can do today to dwell in the shelter of his wings?

"I CAN'T KEEP HIM ALIVE"

Jocelyn

The LORD brings death and makes alive; he brings down
to the grave and raises up.

1 SAMUEL 2:6

"I spend my life just trying to keep my son alive. I am consumed, depleted. I pour out all I am and still it is not enough. Oh, Father God! How does a mother's heart become utterly spent?" Rebekah Benimoff wept as she prayed. And then the answer settled on her heart: "When this mother tries to claim that which is for the hands of God alone."[1]

Keeping her son with multiple medical disorders alive has been Rebekah's goal for more than twelve years. "It has been my pursuit *but it is not my calling.* As if *I* could breathe life and breath and wholeness into his body with all my striving."

Rebekah's words echo the prayer of another mother, uttered thousands of years ago, as Hannah gave her small son Samuel to be raised in the temple by a priest. "The LORD brings death and makes alive; he brings down to the grave and raises up" (1 Sam. 2:6). Job, too, testified to God's life-giving power: "The Spirit of God has made me; the breath of the Almighty gives me life" (Job 33:4).

If it were in her power, Rebekah would sustain her son's life. But it isn't. Neither is it in my power, or in yours, to keep our children with us on earth one day longer than God's plan provides for. Psalm 139:16 tells us, "All the days ordained for me were written in your book before one of them came to be."

"It is our job to love our children, to soothe and serve," said Rebekah. We want to help give them the best life they can possibly have. But it's not our job to keep life in their bodies. That, my friends, is for God alone. To assume otherwise is to hang a crushing responsibility around your neck, one you were never meant to carry. God is the Author of Life (Acts 3:15). We are merely stewards of it.

Let go of your expectations of yourself. These were the words God placed on Rebekah's heart, and they apply to each of us as well. *Let go*—but not of your caregiving, nor of prayer, nor of your fighting for your child to have the best care possible. God is saying to each of us, *Let go of that crushing burden you placed on yourself. You are so weary from straining beneath a weight I never meant for you to have. Come unto me, and I will give you rest. My yoke is easy and my burden is light. Yes, care for my children whom I have placed in your care. But leave the life and death to me.*

"I am certain this will be a process, a journey with many needed reminders," said Rebekah. "But I am also sure that abundant living is not possible without this letting go. God does not expect me to be perfect, He simply asks me to be real and allow the blanket of grace to cover that which I cannot . . . and was never meant to. Here, I find rest for my soul."

Lord, I confess I've taken on burdens that aren't from you. Give me the strength to care for my child the way you want me to, and the courage to leave the outcome up to you. Oh, how I need your grace. Refresh me with the rest that comes from you alone. In Jesus's name, amen.

DIGGING DEEPER

1. What is one expectation you have for yourself that you need to release?

2. If you were to trust God with the number of days your child has, how would your perspective change?

3. What verse from today's reading is the most helpful reminder that our children are God's children who are on loan to us?

THE HARD WORK OF HEALING

Jocelyn

He heals the brokenhearted and binds up their wounds.

PSALM 147:3

Gloria Williams assumed her sixteen-year-old son's sudden illness would be just one more hurdle in his medically complex life. But the fever never came down, even though he was being treated in the hospital. His systems began failing. Doctors began CPR. The paddles jolted his body and shuddered through Gloria as she watched from just a few feet away.

"One of the doctors kept looking at me. He was looking for a signal that it was OK to let him go. Finally, after forty minutes of them trying to bring my son back, I said, 'It's OK.' Then he called it."

There had been no warning, no way to prepare. And though Gloria knew Monroe was now perfectly healthy in body and mind in heaven with Jesus, the gaping hole his absence carved from her heart felt large enough to swallow her whole.

"I begged the Holy Spirit to please just get me through it," said Gloria. "I wanted to shut away the world. But I couldn't. I had to go on for my other kids. How can I tell other people God will see them through if I'm not allowing God to see me through?"

There were times when Gloria's path seemed so hard that she couldn't go another step. But God would give her what she needed when she needed it—a caring person to help or words of comfort to lift her up and encourage her to persevere.

She could have rejected such help and wallowed in her misery; instead, she worked at healing. "When you allow God to work through you, you're working. You're putting your feet on the ground, your hands to the plow. If God is working through you, you're working right alongside him."

And very often, it hurts. Laurie Wallin, whose four daughters include two special-needs children, likens the healing type of pain to when our bodies regain nerve function after a period of numbness. When we feel our wounds again, even as they are being healed, it isn't pleasant! Sometimes, Laurie points out, healing pain hurts worse than wounding pain "because it requires a measure of hope. Of trust in life and process and the possibility of better. . . . It drives us to help others heal too."[2]

Agonizing though it was for Gloria to walk out her faith, the example she provided led Gloria's sister and one of Gloria's daughters to give their lives to the Lord. "People say, 'Oh, that's why your son had to die.' I want to shake them. I don't know why my son died, but I know God didn't have to take him to save my sister and daughter. The only one who had to die was Jesus."

First Peter 2:24 says, "He himself bore our sins in his body on the cross, so that we might die to sins and live for righteousness; 'by his wounds you have been healed.'" While our wounds require healing, Christ's wounds guarantee our healing.

Whether you are grieving a physical death, or your child's brain damage, or the loss of your dreams, you know how easy it is to numb the pain by self-medicating or distract yourself with frantic schedules. We can even pretend we're fine long past the typical denial stage of grief, when really, a piece of us has died inside. Processing our grief hurts. It brings feelings to the surface that we'd rather not feel. But only by working through the grief can we approach healing. God, who knows what it is to lose a Son, and Jesus, a man "familiar with pain" (Isa. 53:3), are with you every step of the way.

> *Lord, I'm suffering right now. Show me the next right step to take so you can bring me to a place of healing. Hold my hand and walk me through it. Give me the courage I need to face life from here on out. In Jesus's name, amen.*

DIGGING DEEPER

1. What is causing the most pain to your heart right now?
2. What are you most afraid of in facing your feelings?
3. Name one step toward healing that you could take this week.

ASKING FOR MORE

Jocelyn

Ask and it will be given to you; seek and you will find;
knock and the door will be opened to you.

MATTHEW 7:7

Laurie Wallin was no stranger to difficult diagnoses. But when the
doctor pointed to her daughter's brain scan from the recent MRI,
a fresh wave of grief crashed over her. "She's missing a third of one of
her frontal lobes," said Laurie. "It's all in the executive function areas.
The moment I saw it, I thought, *I don't know if she's* ever *going to be
independent.*"

The twelve-year-old had already been held back a year in school
and was now entering middle school, even though she could not cope
with fifth grade. Now Laurie learned the girl's Reactive Attachment
Disorder—which caused lying, stealing, and regular wetting and soiling incidents—was only part of the problem. A portion of her child's
brain was missing. And you can't medicate or do therapy with a part of
the brain that isn't there.

"I went through a really depressed place because I couldn't see how
she was going to make it," Laurie said. "I was capable as a kid, I know
what it's like to go into middle school, but I don't have a clue what that's

like for someone who looks like they can but might not be able. It was terrifying and disorienting. I didn't know where we were headed."

Two months later, a light broke through Laurie's darkness. "The point that pulled me out of the grief, was asking for more than I'd ever asked from anyone else, ever." Laurie had been working with seven teachers every week, plus therapists, for her two high-needs daughters, who both need help focusing on homework due to ADHD. On top of that, she also had two typical daughters to raise.

"I'd been able to manage it for years, but my life had become unmanageable. I had to ask for permanent help. So now my husband takes one of the girls for one semester, and I manage the other one. He oversees all her homework and meets with the teachers. My daughter with brain damage and incontinence issues will need more structure and more people involved in her being independent, but maybe that's possible. Maybe I don't have to be the one person who does everything."

Friends, we don't have to do this journey alone. Jesus tells us to ask, seek, and knock, and that we will receive (Matt. 7:7). In Luke 18:1–8, Jesus tells the parable of the persistent widow who pestered an unjust judge until he granted her justice. "Will not God bring about justice for his chosen ones, who cry out to him day and night? Will he keep putting them off?" (v. 7).

Paul wrote, "Do not be anxious about anything, but in every situation, by prayer and petition, with thanksgiving, present your requests to God" (Phil. 4:6).

Not only are we encouraged to ask the Lord for help, but we are to carry each other's burdens as well (Gal. 6:2). Over and over, we are told to love one another. Serving other members in the body of Christ shows the world we are his disciples.

Yet many of us are reluctant to make our needs known. Why? Do we believe we should be able to manage our own families by ourselves? Can't we imagine anyone would be able to help if we asked them to? Are we afraid that if we ask for help, people will think we are bad parents?

Or that no one would believe us when we say parenting kids with special needs is rewarding and fulfilling?

Asking for help made Laurie feel vulnerable and disoriented. But ultimately, it brought hope. Whether it's your child's teachers, your spouse, extended family, church, or friends, don't resist asking for the support you need.

> *Lord, it's hard to admit when I need help. Show me areas in which I could use support, and help me match those needs with the best people or resources. Thank you that you desire to give us good gifts. Help me to humbly receive them. In Jesus's name, amen.*

DIGGING DEEPER
1. How does the idea of asking for help make you feel?
2. In which area of your life could you use more support?
3. Name one thing for which you could ask for help.

CRUSHED SPIRIT

Jocelyn

The human spirit can endure in sickness,
but a crushed spirit who can bear?
PROVERBS 18:14

As a military wife and popular military blogger, Kathryn Sneed knows all about post-traumatic stress disorder. She just never thought she would be diagnosed with it herself.

Caring for her autistic son would have been enough to produce chronic stress at levels similar to those who have experienced combat trauma.Then Kathryn's daughter was born, and almost right away she displayed medical complexities that still elude diagnosis. Severe reflux, failure to thrive, aspiration—at one stage, the choking episodes numbered up to twenty per day.

As more tests came and went, I began to grow numb. The doctors and nurses would tell me they were surprised I wasn't crying and they didn't know how I was so calm. I didn't have time to cry, I had to be strong for my baby. I wasn't calm, on the inside the storm was raging and the numbness just grew.

The anxiety was severe. Any sign of sickness in my kids sent me into a panic attack for thought of something serious and having to stay in the hospital again. . . .

Although the choking episodes had gotten better and were almost non-existent, coughing or choking of any kind in child or adult would send me into a panic. It was like being slammed in the face with everything we had been through with my daughter.[3]

Flashbacks and nightmares haunted her. Several times, chest pains became so severe that she nearly went to the hospital, thinking she was having a heart attack.

In a way, Kathryn was right. Her heart and her spirit had indeed been attacked. Proverbs 18:14 says that during a physical illness, we can keep up our spirits; but, as the King James Version puts it, "a wounded spirit who can bear?" The New International Version calls it a "crushed spirit," and the New American Standard Bible, a "broken spirit." Whether your spirit is wounded, crushed, or broken, it must be cared for to recover.

"Physician, heal thyself": most of us have heard the phrase. But Barb Dittrich, parent of a child with hemophilia and founder of Snappin' Ministries, suggests an alternative: "Caregiver, care also for thyself." Prayer and Scripture are absolutely critical tools in our recovery. Ever since her son was little, she and her son would pray through the verses to help calm both of their spirits before infusions. Prayer at such times is indispensable.

"However, as the number of crises increased, it became apparent we needed more help," Barb wrote. "Sadly, the Church (including us, its members) can forget that in addition to working through prayer and the Word, God also works through people. This includes medical and therapeutic professionals."[4]

Would any of us deny medicine or therapy to our children if we knew it could help them? Would we tell autistic children to "snap out of it" or children with cerebral palsy to "just try harder" to walk without those braces? Of course not. Yet many of us are tempted to deny or talk ourselves out of our own pain. Only when Kathryn and Barb shared with counselors and medical professionals were they able to get help and start experiencing some relief.

Prayer is mission-critical. Spending time in the Word is nonnegotiable. Surrounding yourself with the body of Christ is invaluable. But if you still are experiencing physiological symptoms that interfere with daily life, don't ignore your broken spirit. Seek help from a trusted counselor or mental health professional.[5] "Two are better than one. . . . If either of them falls down, one can help the other up. But pity anyone who falls and has no one to help them up" (Eccl. 4:9–10).

Lord, give me the courage to admit when I need someone to help me up. Guide me to the right people and resources. Great Physician, bring healing to my spirit, and bind up my broken heart. In Jesus's name, amen.

Digging Deeper

1. On a scale of one to ten, how would you rate the anxiety you feel on a daily basis?
2. What makes your anxiety worse, and what brings you calm and comfort?
3. At what point would you consider seeking counseling?

LOSS AND THE HOPE OF HEAVEN

Kimberly

In all their distress he too was distressed,
and the angel of his presence saved them. In his love and
mercy he redeemed them; he lifted them up and carried
them all the days of old.

ISAIAH 63:9

When our daughter Abbey was born, her delivery was a few seconds short of tragic. She suffers multiple disabilities as a result of that day. Although the Lord was gracious to us in sparing her life, I did lose the life I thought I was going to live and the life I thought she was going to live.

Eight years later my husband and I gave birth to our stillborn son, Jackson. As the nurse wheeled me out of the maternity ward, I left carrying a small remembrance box instead of my baby. Instead of picking out clothes, I picked out funeral details. And nothing, absolutely nothing, prepares you to sit across from a tiny casket. It felt like some horrific dream I could not wake up from. I had trouble sleeping; my only comfort was God's Word and his promises.

Dealing with the loss of a loved one, or the loss associated with the diagnosis of our child, is painful, and healing takes time. What do we do while we are going through it? I believe we go back to the beginning.

In God's Word we find that sickness and death originally came into the world as a result of sin (Gen. 3). In the perfect world we were meant to live in, there was no sickness, disability, or the grief that accompanies death. Our longing for things to be the way they were meant to be is proof of our desire for heaven. Ecclesiastes 3:11 says, "He has made everything beautiful in its time. He has also set eternity in the human heart; yet no one can fathom what God has done from beginning to end."

But we have hope, because Christ came to restore things to the way they were meant to be and, praise God, the way they *will* be again one day. In Revelation 21 we read about a new heaven and earth where God himself will once again dwell with his people. In this new reality, "He will wipe away every tear from their eyes, and death shall be no more, neither shall there be mourning, nor crying, nor pain anymore, for the former things have passed away" (v. 4 ESV).

While we wait for these promises to become our reality, during sleepless nights or times of aching sadness, we can recall verses like Psalm 63:6–8: "I remember you upon my bed, and meditate on you in the watches of the night; for you have been my help, and in the shadow of your wings I will sing for joy. My soul clings to you; your right hand upholds me" (ESV). What a poignant reminder that even as we long to hold on to what or whom we have lost, our heavenly Father is holding on to us. May we cling to him with all the strength we can muster, and trust him to carry us through.

The rest of the world will move on long before we're ready to do so. After the condolence cards have stopped filling our mailboxes and the emails and phone calls slow down, we can know with confidence that our pain still matters to God. Not only does he feel our distress (Isa. 63:9) but he records it. "You have kept count of my tossings; put my tears in your bottle. Are they not in your book?" (Ps. 56:8 ESV). Not one tear has gone unnoticed. Every aspect of our suffering matters to God.

Only God can heal our wounds from loss. He himself is the balm that covers our broken hearts. The emotional scars will be a reminder of what we've lost, but they are also a reminder of God's sustaining grace and the promise of heaven.

Jesus, I ask you to be my comforter as I face each trial and loss while I am raising my child. You are intimately acquainted with grief, and I know that mine matters to you. Help me run to you with my doubts and fears and sadness. Be my sustainer, my strength, and my great hope. In Jesus's name, amen.

DIGGING DEEPER
1. What Scriptures give you peace about loss?
2. If you are grieving a diagnosis or fearing the loss of your child, how can you find hope in Christ?
3. What mature Christian believer can you share these fears and thoughts with?

HUDDLE UP

Jocelyn

Praise be to the God and Father of our Lord Jesus Christ,
the Father of compassion and the God of all comfort,
who comforts us in all our troubles, so that we can
comfort those in any trouble with the comfort
we ourselves receive from God.

2 CORINTHIANS 1:3-4

People grieve in different ways and at different paces. One person's grief will rarely match his or her spouse's grief exactly, and that's all right. It's not all right, however, to try to walk through that valley completely on one's own. If you're mourning a loss of some kind, whether it's a diagnosis or a death or anything in between, it's time to huddle up.

In her book *A Different Dream for My Child*, Jolene Philo calls grief a team sport. "Players are drafted onto the team, not because they're winners, but because they've lost so much," she wrote. "The goal of the game varies from day to day. Sometimes the goal is to get out of bed in the morning. Sometimes the goal is to put one foot ahead of the other throughout the day. Sometimes the goal is to breathe, to eat, to feel, to hope. But the players can't meet their goals alone. Because grief's a team sport, and team members only win by sticking together."[6]

Before Gloria Williams lost her son Monroe, she had watched her best friend lose a son. "Watching her go through her grief, I saw how she was able to carry on. So I had somebody who really showed an example of strong faith and what it really meant. When we're in the valley, everything we believe and say all comes together and you have to decide, 'Is God really sovereign? Is this really the Lord's will?' I always did believe the answer was yes."

Watching her best friend come to the same conclusion in her own grief bolstered Gloria, even before she knew how much she would need it. "She is my mentoring Christian and my best friend. The Lord was kind to me in that he prepared me even when I didn't know it. It was very hard still, but that was amazing."

Your own best friend may not be able to relate to you as perfectly as Gloria's did to her. But it's still important to find someone who can walk with you on the journey. It may very well be your spouse who links arms with you. It could be your pastor or a counselor. Or another bereaved parent may bring you the comfort and understanding he or she already knows you need.

"If you have lost a child or are facing such a loss, you need to let people join your team," Jolene wrote. "Don't huddle alone on the sidelines, wrapped in a blanket of grief, isolated by the pain of your injuries. The only way to get from where you are today to where you need to be one day in the future is to become a team player, to let other parents who lost children into your life."[7]

The apostle Paul wrote, "Praise be to the God and Father of our Lord Jesus Christ, the Father of compassion and the God of all comfort, who comforts us in all our troubles, so that we can comfort those in any trouble with the comfort we ourselves receive from God. For just as we share abundantly in the sufferings of Christ, so also our comfort abounds through Christ" (2 Cor. 1:3–5). The Father of compassion and the God of all comfort is true to his name. Let others who have already experienced his comfort now bring that comfort to you.

Lord, show me your compassion. When I am too weary to seek comfort from your Word, bring me comfort through your people. Remind me of your presence, even when I don't feel it. Give me the grace to let others on my team. In Jesus's name, amen.

Digging Deeper

1. When you are grieving a loss, with whom do you share your feelings?

2. Among your friends and acquaintances, who may be able to relate well to your experience?

3. Which thoughts and truths might you share someday to comfort someone else?

THE TOWEL

Kimberly

Humble yourselves before the Lord, and he will lift you up.

JAMES 4:10

There was a point in time when the social gap between Abbey and her peer group began to widen. Suddenly they were no longer chubby-cheeked toddlers in the nursery learning to share toys. Soon my friends would start to complain about their children's "attitudes" and discipline issues, and all I could think was, I would take a little sass now and then if it meant Abbey could talk. Now that she is even older, my husband can barely stand to watch a father/daughter dance at weddings. He said to me after a wedding this summer, "That was my moment. That's the one I was supposed to have but I will never get." The milestones never stop coming, and each one that passes us by can be a painful reminder.

Carly Nicodemus has four children, two of whom have nonhered-itary, unrelated genetic disorders. When one son was going through a series of tests and treatments for his disorder, both her sisters had babies. "Dealing with a child who has a genetic disorder while at the same time seeing a regular stream of photos of healthy babies—that was even harder than the diagnosis," Carly said. She offers a suggestion for others who, like her, may struggle in this area. "Try not to do the comparison game because that will eat you up in so many ways. Focus on the little victories, the areas that you and your child are flourishing in."

Focusing on the little victories is key. As our peer group's children meet milestone after milestone, we have to narrow our focus. Like switching from a panoramic lens on our camera to a close-up lens, we can learn to thrive exactly where God has us. At Taylor University, President Jay Kessler used to remind us all the time to "bloom where you are planted." Those words have helped Ryan and me to release the unmet milestones and focus on where God has us now instead.

And where are we? We are serving our children. Some of us will physically care for our children for the rest of their lives, or the rest of ours. At our graduation ceremony from Taylor University, we received not only our diplomas but also a beloved towel. The towel is a reminder to live like Christ, with a heart for service.

In John 13 we see Jesus and his disciples preparing for the Passover Feast. The King of Kings removed his outer garments and assumed the station of lowly household servant as he began to wash the disciples' feet. Dusty sandals were untied, and dirty feet were exposed and washed clean by the hands of Christ. In just a matter of days, Jesus would humbly bare himself again, this time on the cross. His righteousness would expose the filth of our sin to be washed clean by his blood.

Jesus explained that what he did for the disciples, we should do for one another. "Now that I, your Lord and Teacher, have washed your feet, you also should wash one another's feet. I have set you an example that you should do as I have done for you. Very truly I tell you, no servant is greater than his master, nor is a messenger greater than the one who sent him. Now that you know these things, you will be blessed if you do them" (John 13:14–17).

As we focus on where God has us, we learn to let go of where we will never be and can begin to thrive where we are in a life of humble service to God and to our children (James 4:10). We can begin to learn what it means to deny ourselves and take up our cross daily and follow him (Luke 9:23). As Jesus said, we will be blessed if we do these things.

Father, you understand every milestone that my child will never meet and every victory we will celebrate instead. Help me to bloom where you've planted me and to live a life of humble service to you and to my child. In Jesus's name, amen.

DIGGING DEEPER
1. What milestones can you give over to the Lord today?
2. How can you narrow the lens of how you view your child's achievements?
3. What does Christ's humble service and sacrifice mean to you?

FROM DARKNESS INTO LIGHT

Jocelyn

Let the one who walks in the dark, who has no light,
trust in the name of the LORD and rely on their God.

ISAIAH 50:10

"So, do you have children?" The polite question opened raw wounds for Alane Pearce, who had trained herself to answer, "Not right now." Alane didn't mean that someday she might have a child. The truth was, she had eight children already. All of them were in heaven.

During the span of five years, Alane lost seven unborn children and a two-week-old son who died due to a heart defect. It took another five years of conversations with God for her to emerge from the darkness of grief and depression. Once she did, she realized how much she had adapted to living "in the dark."

"For someone dealing with the death of a loved one, this is how life seems; we walk around in the darkness for a while, but soon our eyes adjust," she wrote in *Faith Deployed . . . Again*. "Eventually we forget that there can be light. We may even find that we like the darkness and want to stay. Trouble is, if we do, we will draw farther away from the One who brings the light."[8]

Jesus knew this. He warned, "Are there not twelve hours of daylight?

Anyone who walks in the daytime will not stumble, for they see by this world's light. It is when a person walks at night that they stumble, for they have no light" (John 11:9–10). Those of us in spiritual or emotional darkness can find light in the Scriptures: "The unfolding of your words gives light" (Ps. 119:130). Jesus himself is light: "I am the light of the world. Whoever follows me will never walk in darkness, but will have the light of life" (John 8:12).

Psalm 84:11 says that "the LORD God is a sun and shield." "When I am fighting off the dark places that people with depression and grief are haunted by, I call on God to become my sun and shield," Alane wrote in her memoir, *Notes from the Margins*. "God is my sun shining in the dark places to warm my weary spirit, and my shield to fight off the fiery darts of the devil who tries very hard to separate me from God again."[9]

If you're grieving a loss of any kind, remember that though you may feel lost and alone, God does not desire for you to be alone. For this reason, he sent his Son, "the light of all mankind. The light shines in the darkness, and the darkness has not overcome it" (John 1:4–5). Yes, darkness refers to sin. But when sin entered the world, so did disease, disorders, and death. When we have Jesus in our lives, we have light. We need not stumble about blindly. We may walk through the darkest valley, but not alone (Ps. 23:4). We need not dwell in our dark places.

"Beloved, you honor the memory of your loved one by embracing that light," wrote Alane. "Allow Jesus to shine into your darkness. Let Him help you grieve and lead you with His comfort. Let Him guide your feet into the path of peace. Peace with your grief. Peace with your life. Peace with God. Then you will have the strength to 'declare the praises of him who called you out of the darkness and into his wonderful light' (1 Peter 2:9)."[10]

Lord, be my sun and my shield. Shine your light into my darkness. Protect me from the attacks of the Evil One. Allow me to feel the warmth of your light on my face once again. In Jesus's name, amen.

Digging Deeper

1. Have you grown accustomed to walking around in the dark? What sources bring light to your darkness?

2. Which of the verses in this devotional can you pray aloud when you have no words of your own to offer?

3. Which of Satan's lies have you bought into? What does the Bible say instead?

WHAT DO WE DO WITH GOD?

Jocelyn

I cry out to You for help, but You do not answer me;
I stand up, and You turn Your attention against me.
You have become cruel to me; with the might of Your
hand You persecute me. You lift me up to the wind and
cause me to ride; and You dissolve me in a storm.

JOB 30:20–22 (NASB)

God is holy and good, and "there is no wickedness in him" (Ps. 92:15). And yet, sometimes it doesn't feel that way at all.

Kathryn Sneed admits she's been angry at God. She still struggles with it. Her first baby was miscarried. Her firstborn was diagnosed with autism and sensory processing disorder as a toddler, and her second child has had severe medical challenges since birth.

"There is no road map for what you are supposed to do if you feel this way," she wrote on her blog. "You are not supposed to be angry at God. And even as I thought about it I was waiting for lightning to come down and strike me."[11]

For two years, Rebekah Benimoff held in "an enormous amount of devastation over my son's diagnosis, and the burden of caring for his medical needs. My dream of a healthy child had been lost. I'd blamed God for this loss, though at the time I had not even realized it."

The question cannot be avoided: If God can heal my child(ren)— and he can!— why does he choose not to? Or for some of us: Why did he take my child from this earth so soon?

"We can't technically forgive God, but we *must do something with* Him, with His sovereignty, with His hand in all of this," wrote Laurie Wallin in *Get Your Joy Back*.[12] So when we're grieving, what do we *do* with God?

Be angry. Let God hear it. Laurie's own "angry phase" began when, instead of bringing her daughter home from the psychiatric hospital which was to treat her reactive attachment disorder behaviors, she instead needed to take her to a residential facility to live for who knew how long. "I swore, screamed, and wept. . . . [I turned] the full fury of my grief toward the only One who *could* do anything about any of this . . . but hadn't."[13]

When we vent our feelings to the One who already knows them, we're in good company. Jacob's wrestling match with God was quite literal (see Gen. 32), but other heroes of the faith, such as Elijah, Moses, Abraham, and David have grappled fiercely as well.

Only when we let ourselves fight with God do "we find ourselves close enough to hear Him . . . [which] places us close enough that, when we're spent and collapse into depression, we fall into the only arms that can really console us in our grief and loss," wrote Laurie.[14]

And when our anger is finally spent? It's time to allow God to reveal himself to us and experience the truth that not only is he sovereign, but God is also love itself (1 John 4:8).

"Though it took me two years to fully embrace him, I was finally able to face the grief, but only with him gently drawing me through the healing process," said Rebekah. "Despite my questions, he wants to walk with me—if I will only allow him in."

What about you? Have you come to the end of yourself? Is it time to face God and yell at him? Or are you ready to sink into his arms, exhausted? Either way, he's ready.

Lord God, you already know my thoughts and feelings, but help me to honestly express myself to you, even if it isn't pretty. Give me the courage to face you again and again. Show yourself to me. In Jesus's name, amen.

DIGGING DEEPER
1. What are you angry about right now?
2. What thoughts and feelings do you need to share with God?
3. Are you willing to pour out your true feelings to God? Why or why not?

FIVE

Drenched
Nourishing the Soul

The LORD is my shepherd, I lack nothing.
He makes me lie down in green pastures,
he leads me beside quiet waters,
he refreshes my soul.

PSALM 23:1-3

A FAMILY WHO WORSHIPS

Kimberly

Ascribe to the LORD, O families of the peoples,
ascribe to the LORD glory and strength! Ascribe to
the LORD the glory due his name; bring an offering,
and come into his courts! Worship the LORD in the
splendor of holiness; tremble before him, all the earth!

PSALM 96:7-9 (ESV)

As the parent of a child with special needs, you have most likely discovered all the obstacles to getting to church—and staying in it!—that our family has. When our daughter was old enough to be in a Sunday school class, we found ourselves in a difficult place. Should I go to class with her as her aid? What about her physical needs, snack "issues," attention span? Though we attended a reasonably sized congregation, there was no program in place to support us as a family with a special-needs child in our desire to faithfully attend worship.

I came to a real crossroads. Either I kept her with me all the time, or we stayed home, or I had to find people who were willing to work with her. I can't tell you how desperately I needed an hour at church to be with the Lord without the distraction and demands of my sweet girl.

Perhaps you find yourself in a similar position. There are frustrations

147

and obstacles that will stand in the way of attending corporate worship when you have a child with special needs. Psalm 96:7–9 reminds us that we are to ascribe to the Lord glory and strength, to bring our offerings, and to come into his courts. His holiness and glory call us to worship.

The fourth of the Ten Commandments is to remember the Sabbath and keep it holy. Hebrews 10:25 says that we should "not giv[e] up meeting together, as some are in the habit of doing, but encourag[e] one another—and all the more as you see the Day approaching." Clearly it is important to God that we participate in worshipping him. We need to attend church not because we want to get something out of it (though I always leave feeling better than when I came) but because we are called to it. He commands it and deserves it. Corporate worship is one of the ways that we can give back to the Lord for all he's done for us.

I love the phrase from Psalm 96, "O families of the peoples." I'm sure your special child is a big part of your family, but he or she is also a part of the family of God. We fight for our children's daily routines at school, for the best medical treatment, and for their growth and development. We work so hard to ensure their well-being, often at the expense of our own. One way that we can build up our children, ourselves, and the family of God is to participate in a church body. If you find yourself without a church home or frequently absent from church because of your child's needs, remember God's calling to worship, and work to make changes in your life and congregation so you can attend. You *will* be blessed!

> *Father, forgive me for not making time to worship you with others in the body of Christ. You are worthy of all the glory and honor and praise that is due your name. Give me the portion of grace and strength I need in order to faithfully attend church. In Jesus's name, amen.*

DIGGING DEEPER

1. What issues make church attendance difficult for your family?
2. What value do you find in being part of a church family?
3. Whom could you talk to on your church's leadership staff to try to improve the experience that families with special needs will have at your church?

SPEAK LIFE

Jocelyn

The soothing tongue is a tree of life,
but a perverse tongue crushes the spirit.
PROVERBS 15:4

Jeff Davidson and his teenaged son Jon Alex, who has autism and cerebral palsy, have a nightly ritual. After dinner, Jeff helps Jon Alex onto his platform swing and pushes him while singing to him for forty-five minutes or until Jon Alex is ready for bed. Between the songs, Jeff intersperses prayers and blessings for his nonverbal son.

The last thing Jon Alex hears before he drifts off to sleep every night is the voice of his father: "You are the best son in the whole wide world and I wouldn't want any other boy but you, because God made you for me, and God made me for you."[1]

Our words matter. For better or for worse, what we say makes a difference. "The tongue has the power of life and death" (Prov. 18:21). Jesus spoke and raised Lazarus from the dead; he cursed a fig tree and it withered immediately. While the power of physical life is reserved for God alone, our own words can breathe emotional and spiritual life into another or cause someone's spirit to shrivel and cease to bear fruit.

"Your child with special needs is your fig tree," Jeff writes. "Every time you pass by or encounter your child, you need to speak words of life, love, and affirmation over your child or children."[2]

Your spouse is a fig tree as well. Especially during times of great stress, your words can either nourish or wither your spouse and your marriage. For example, soon after Laura Slezak's daughter was diagnosed with Angelman syndrome, she dedicated a blog post to affirming her husband Craig's many contributions to the family, such as working two jobs, spending time with the family (even night shifts with the baby), helping with housework, listening to Laura, and making his wife and kids laugh.[3]

"Laura's blog post really lifted me up, especially when she named the reasons she called me the 'best daddy ever,'" Craig said. "She made it specific, which tells me she notices. And for that, I felt pretty great." Words of life are powerful, whether spoken in private or publicly.

What we tell ourselves makes a difference too. In the beginning of Psalm 42, David cries out to God that his tears have been his food. But by the end, he's talking to himself: "Why, my soul, are you downcast? Why so disturbed within me? Put your hope in God, for I will yet praise him, my Savior and my God" (v. 11). Praising the Lord aloud speaks life to others and to ourselves.

This was never as clear to Jeff as the night Jon Alex was so exhausted he decided to skip the swing-sing session and head straight for bed. Jeff realized then just how important that time had been for his own state of mind. Without it, he was agitated and restless.

"This was where I forgot all about my cares and concerns and focused on what really mattered. This is where I feel closest to God and his purpose for my life. I have come to crave and need those moments with him and that bedroom swing far more than Jon Alex does."[4] What had begun as therapy for Jon Alex had become therapy for Jeff as well.

Words matter. "The words of the reckless pierce like swords, but the tongue of the wise brings healing" (Prov. 12:18). May we carefully choose words that nourish the soul: our children's, our spouse's, and our own.

Lord, help me tame my tongue. Help me use it to steer myself, my children, and my spouse along paths of gratitude and encouragement. Fill me with your Spirit so that my words may bring life and healing. In Jesus's name, amen.

DIGGING DEEPER

1. What can you tell your spouse that would speak life to him or her?
2. What words of life can you share with your child(ren)?
3. How can you speak life to yourself?

LACK OF SLEEP IS A FORM OF TORTURE

Kimberly

I lift up my eyes to the mountains—where does my
help come from? My help comes from the LORD, the
Maker of heaven and earth. He will not let your foot slip—
he who watches over you will not slumber; indeed, he
who watches over Israel will neither slumber nor sleep.

PSALM 121:1-4

There are hours of the night that bring out the worst in me. When Abbey came home from the NICU as a baby, we were up every few hours for months on end. When we have a medical crisis, we find ourselves back to that grueling newborn schedule.

Many of you can relate. Rob Wurzel describes a similar time. "For eight months after Reagan's metabolic crisis, we averaged about four hours of broken sleep each night. We were in survival mode. There wasn't much time for anything else. Life was pretty terrible, there were plenty of times I wanted to give up or run away."

During one of my stretches of no sleep, my daughter's pediatrician said to me, "You know, all over the world they use lack of sleep as a form of torture. It clinically messes with your brain. Do whatever you need to do to get some sleep."

Sometimes our lack of sleep comes from our trying to keep our children alive. Other times we are up in the night to feed not our children but our worries. During these times, we must physically, emotionally, and spiritually submit to the Lord.

During one hospital stay with Abbey, I found it difficult to sleep even though she was being monitored and the nurses were up all night checking on her. It was then that Psalm 121:1–4 came to mind. God is in control. I let my body surrender to sleep knowing that God himself neither slumbers nor sleeps. He would keep watch on her all night. In truth, he watches over every second of her life. There is no amount of worry that can change the outcome of whatever stressor or crisis we are facing. In Matthew 6:27, Jesus asks, "Can any one of you by worrying add a single hour to your life?"

Rob practices reading through the Psalms to get through difficult times, and I have a friend who keeps verses on worry and anxiety on her phone. Any way that we can grab on to Scripture will keep our minds in a place to receive the peace of God. Turning things over to God releases us from the strain of trying to control them ourselves. Rob shared, "It's when I am pressed, when everything is crashing down around me, when nothing seems to be going right, when my nightmares become reality, when nothing I can do can change anything around me . . . that is when I find myself closest to God. That is when I turned everything over to him to survive."

Philippians 4:6–7 is a beautiful reminder of how to submit to God. "Do not be anxious about anything, but in every situation, by prayer and petition, with thanksgiving, present your requests to God. And the peace of God, which transcends all understanding, will guard your hearts and your minds in Christ Jesus." When sleep evades you, recall these verses spoken by Jesus in Matthew 11:28–30, "Come to me, all you who are weary and burdened, and I will give you rest. Take my yoke upon you and learn from me, for I am gentle and humble in heart, and you will find rest for your souls. For my yoke is easy and my burden is light."

Father God, help me to find emotional, mental, physical, and spiritual rest in you. Help me to rest, knowing that you neither slumber nor sleep, that you hold all things in your hands. Guard my mind against thoughts that would keep me awake. Help me to reach out to others for help if I am not getting enough physical rest. In Jesus's name, amen.

DIGGING DEEPER

1. Are you getting enough sleep?
2. What steps can you take to ensure that you are not putting your body through a form of torture called sleep deprivation?
3. What verses do you use to find comfort and peace?

STRENGTH FOR THE FIGHT

Kimberly

Even youths grow tired and weary, and young men stumble
and fall; but those who hope in the LORD will renew their
strength. They will soar on wings like eagles; they will run
and not grow weary, they will walk and not be faint.

ISAIAH 40:30-31

Taking care of a child with special needs requires more energy and
strength than any other job I undertake. There have been times
when I just couldn't face my own weaknesses. Some days it feels like
an uphill battle. If any of us are going to have strength for the fight, we
need to be like well-trained soldiers. We need reinforcements. And we
need access to and resources from our commanding officer.

Personally, I've had to train myself with better self-care. As Abbey
has gotten older, my weight gain has made it difficult to care for her
needs. I have not always taken care of my physical body. Over the
last three years I've worked hard to create new habits that will help
to heal my own body, so that I have the strength to take care of hers.
First Corinthians 6:19–20 is transforming the way I care for myself.
It reads, "Do you not know that your bodies are temples of the Holy
Spirit, who is in you, whom you have received from God? You are not

your own; you were bought at a price. Therefore honor God with your bodies."

We must care for our own physical and spiritual needs in order to build and maintain the strength this lifestyle requires. We also need reinforcements in our lives, sometimes desperately! The trouble is making that clear. Wendy Hilton understands exactly what that's like. She wrote,

> Nobody realized that things *really had* gotten to be too much for me to handle alone. Until one day I crashed. I completely fell apart.
>
> Looking back, I can see that I wasn't making myself clear. My family and friends simply thought I needed reassurance and encouragement. They didn't realize I was warning them that I literally. could. not. keep. going. any. longer. I tried to explain to them in words what I needed, but I couldn't. I really couldn't quite admit it to myself, and I certainly couldn't figure out how to put it into words for someone else to hear. So I gave up. I quit trying to explain it to them.[5]

It takes humility to say to your friends and family, "I need help. I'm drowning. I'm exhausted." When recruiting reinforcements, name what you need from them as specifically as you can. Need someone to mow your lawn? A shoulder to cry on? Time with a Christian counselor? A night at a hotel for one single full night's sleep? Do you need to train a babysitter how to use your child's medical equipment so you can get out of the house? Say so.

Ultimately, we need to look to God, our commander in chief, for strength and guidance. He promises to deliver. I have to continue to look to the Lord for my strength. Philippians 4:19 assures us, "My God will meet all your needs according to the riches of his glory in Christ Jesus." Isaiah 40:29 tells us, "He gives strength to the weary and increases the power of the weak."

As we take the time to care for our physical bodies, to humbly communicate our needs to others, and to look to God for our every need, we will find him giving us the strength for the fight. The battle will continue to be a part of our reality, but there's no need to go into it alone. May we echo the words of Deborah when she said, "O my soul, march on with strength" (Judg. 5:21 NASB).

> *Dear Jesus, help me to look for you when I need strength for this fight. I know you supply all of my needs and see my weariness. Thank you for loving me. I know you'll get me through this. In Jesus's name, amen.*

DIGGING DEEPER

1. In what ways do you feel you lack what you need to care for your child?
2. How can you look to Christ to meet those needs?
3. Are there people and other resources you need to take advantage of to better care for yourself?

HELD TOGETHER

Jocelyn

He is before all things, and in him all things hold together.

COLOSSIANS 1:17

Sharon and Brian Carlson were exhausted. Their schedule was dominated by therapies, appointments, and IEP meetings. They felt isolated from friends. He slept a lot. She yelled a lot. He put in long hours at work. She put her fist through the wall.

Their marriage was in crisis. "We had an actual irreconcilable difference," she said. "Only he wasn't in a place where he could recognize it." Sharon's mom, dad, stepdad, and church all rallied around the Carlsons while wondering, for six months, whether the marriage was going to survive.

What they didn't know then was that Brian has Asperger's. "That's why he could not participate with me and engage in the family the way I wanted him to," Sharon said. The crying spells of the daughter with bipolar, and the wetting and soiling incidents of the daughter with reactive attachment disorder, trigger Brian's need to self-soothe. For him, that means working longer hours and focusing on his laptop once he's home. Now that they know this, the family dynamics are easier to understand.

Still, partnering in marriage while parenting high-needs children is difficult when one spouse also needs accommodation. It's also not uncommon. Neither is it hopeless.

As believers, we get to tap into God's supernatural strength and grace not just for our children but also for our spouse. With our spouse, we can practice patience, forgiveness, love, self-control, humility, gentleness, and kindness. When we falter, we can ask for forgiveness and let God lift us up to try again.

God knew this would wear us out. He speaks to this in Paul's letter to the Galatians: "Let us not become weary in doing good, for at the proper time we will reap a harvest if we do not give up" (6:9). Just what "good" is Paul referring to here? According to John Piper, "Probably the fruit of the Spirit in Galatians 5:22 is the best answer: don't grow weary of being patient and kind and good and faithful and gentle and self-controlled. Don't grow weary of manifesting your peace and joy in all kinds of acts of love to your neighbors and associates and family. In short, don't lose heart in spending yourself through love."[6]

Sometimes, though, we do grow weary in our marriages. Seek counseling or coaching from a pastor or someone you trust. "Whatever you do, find a space that gives you a safe place to fight, reconnect, and heal *together* instead of growing apart," Laurie Wallin wrote in her book *Get Your Joy Back*. "On the same topic, censor ignorant marital advice (i.e., ignore naysayers). Surround yourself with people who value your marriage as much as you do, and graciously decline input from those who don't."[7]

Has your marriage been a casualty of your battle to meet your child's needs? There is hope. God can redeem it. Remember that your spouse is not the enemy. The enemy is the one who would love nothing more than to break apart your family.

"We need polio braces for us to walk our lives together," said Sharon of her marriage. "So we're meeting with our pastor once a month, indefinitely." The point is not that without the braces the marriage might fall apart. The point is that with those supports, walking through life together is possible. In Christ, "all things hold together" (Col. 1:17), including our marriages. Find the support you and your spouse need, and move forward as a team.

> *Lord, help me to not become weary of doing good. As I spend energy on my children, please help me reserve some for my spouse. If our marriage could use support, help us seek it out before we're on the verge of falling apart. Thank you for valuing our marriage so much. In Jesus's name, amen.*

Digging Deeper
1. What is one thing you need to ask of your spouse?
2. What is one thing you could be doing better for your spouse?
3. Identify one possible support to explore for your family.

CONTAGIOUS JOY

Kimberly

The LORD is my strength and my shield; my heart trusts
in him, and he helps me. My heart leaps for joy,
and with my song I praise him.
PSALM 28:7

We sneak around on tiptoe and quickly duck behind a door or crouch behind a couch. Someone counts to ten and yells, "Go!" and we hear her coming. Her flat-footed gait can be heard stomping down the hall along with that inhaled vocalization she does when she's so excited she can't stand it. She looks in the usual places and squeals with delight when she finds a little brother. But the best part of the game is when it's her turn to hide. Sometimes she will go to the last spot where she found someone, but usually she finds a blanket and throws it over herself. Not in a corner or by a bed, though. She sits in the middle of the floor or hallway. She can't take it—she starts to laugh, though she knows she's supposed to be quiet. The boys tiptoe around her and say, "Where is Abbey? I can't find her!" Out of her comes this unmistakable Abbey chuckle, the sound of laughter ready to explode like lava out of a volcano. When they rip the blanket off of her, she can no longer take it and lays completely flat on the floor laughing hysterically. It's completely contagious. Before we know it, we're all laughing with her.

Psalm 126:2–3 is a picture of this kind of contagious, spilling over of joy and laughter: "Our mouths were filled with laughter, our tongues with songs of joy. Then it was said among the nations, 'The Lord has done great things for them.' The Lord has done great things for us, and we are filled with joy."

The Jewish people would sing this and other psalms of ascent together as they traveled toward Jerusalem to celebrate any of three yearly festivals. Why were they so filled with joy and laughter? Because the Lord had done great things for them. Just as my family can't ignore Abbey, blanket-draped in the middle of the room, you and I can't deny our circumstances. And we don't need to. We don't have to cover them up or pretend they aren't there, because despite the hardships, the Lord has done *great* things for us. We can experience blessing and struggle at the same time. Joy in the Lord transcends our frail bodies and feeble minds. Joy is full of God, and emptied of ourselves.

Joy is one of the fruits of the Holy Spirit in our lives (Gal. 5:22), and it's found in the very presence of God. "You make known to me the path of life; you will fill me with joy in your presence, with eternal pleasures at your right hand" (Ps. 16:11).

Like Abbey being uncovered and found by her brothers, in the presence of God we can be completely unveiled and real. When we feel lost or misplaced in this world, his presence reminds us that we are found in Christ. Joy awaits. Psalm 21:6 reads, "Surely you have granted him unending blessings and made him glad with the joy of your presence."

The church in Thessalonica understood this kind of joy. Paul wrote to them, "You became imitators of us and of the Lord, for you welcomed the message in the midst of severe suffering with the joy given by the Holy Spirit. And so you became a model to all the believers in Macedonia and Achaia. The Lord's message rang out from you not only in Macedonia and Achaia—your faith in God has become known everywhere. Therefore we do not need to say anything about it" (1 Thess. 1:6–8). Despite severe suffering, the gospel permeated the lives of the Thessalonian believers with joy from the Holy Spirit and spread out like wildfire. Their faith in God became known everywhere.

Our joy and contentment in Christ can do the same. When we celebrate and meditate on the works of God and enjoy his presence, our joy in Christ can spill over like Abbey's laughter—too pure and beautiful to ignore, too inviting to turn away, so very full and contagious.

Thank you, Lord, for all the moments of laughter and joy that you give me. Thank you for the joy that I can have in you despite my circumstances. Help me to be so full of you that joy overflows and becomes contagious. In Jesus's name, amen.

Digging Deeper

1. When was the last time you laughed with your child?
2. Can you recall a time when someone's joy and cheerful heart was contagious?
3. What reasons do you have for the joy that is found in Christ, and how does this remain despite your circumstances?

COMPASSIONATE FATHER

Kimberly

But you, Lord, are a compassionate and gracious God,
slow to anger, abounding in love and faithfulness.

PSALM 86:15

Our table is set for dinner, and Abbey's equipment is out. A slew of feeding adaptations allows her to participate in our meal independently. The process of using these special tools began when, as an infant, she would gag and choke on anything other than a bottle. She has worked so hard just to swallow properly, not to mention master holding a spoon and getting it to her mouth. Even after all this time, it's still not pretty. There is often food everywhere, all over her and the table in front of her.

As I watch her trying to do this simple task, I well up with compassion for her, because I know how hard it is for her. I want to do anything and everything I can to help her, and I won't give up on her. With compassion, patience, and love we encourage her to keep trying.

As much compassion as I feel for her, it is nothing compared to the love and compassion that God shows us. Jesus knew what it was like to well with compassion for his children. As he looked out at the crowds of people, hungry and in need of physical and spiritual healing, he could not turn them away (Matt. 9:36; 15:32). Like Abbey trying to feed herself, they were helpless and in need of teaching. And so are we. How comforting that God knows how hard it is for us to learn his lessons! But rather than tapping his foot impatiently, arms crossed in frustration, he remains with us and feels our struggle as we try. "As a father has compassion on his children, so the LORD has compassion on those who fear him; for he knows how we are formed, he remembers that we are dust" (Ps. 103:13–14).

He not only knows our weaknesses because he formed us from the dust, but he shows patience beyond imagination. When Moses was on Mount Sinai receiving the second set of stone tablets, the Lord "passed in front of Moses, proclaiming, 'The LORD, the LORD, the compassionate and gracious God, slow to anger, abounding in love and faithfulness'" (Exod. 34:6). Nothing can separate us from that love (Rom. 8:38–39). It is unfailing and perfect (Ps. 52:8; 1 John 4:18), an everlasting love (Jer. 31:3).

Full of compassion, slow to anger, and abounding in love our Father watches us struggle to learn the things of God. Just as Abbey can't help but make a mess when she eats, sometimes we make a big mess of things in our own life and all around us. But God is faithful to forgive. First John 1:9 says, "If we confess our sins, he is faithful and just and will forgive us our sins and purify us from all unrighteousness." It's his forgiveness and purification that give us the strength to keep trying. While we struggle and fight and press on to learn to live a life worthy of Christ, he does not give up on us. We can be "confident of this, that he who began a good work in [us] will carry it on to completion until the day of Christ Jesus" (Phil. 1:6).

Maybe today your struggle is with patience, kindness, or self-control. Maybe you're trying with all your might to look for the good in this season of your life, but bitterness creeps in. Whatever the area in which you may feel you're falling short, remember that God is not watching you in judgment but with compassion. Our Father in heaven will continue to patiently, lovingly help us to be what he's called us to be.

Father, your compassion for me brings me to my knees in thankfulness. You are holy and perfect, slow to anger, and abounding in love. Help me to find rest in your unchanging character despite my flaws and failures. In Jesus's name, amen.

DIGGING DEEPER

1. In what ways does your child cause you to feel compassion?
2. How do you think your compassion for your child compares to God's compassion for you?
3. As you experience the Lord's compassion for you, in what ways can you show that compassion to yourself and others?

SIBLING THERAPY

Jocelyn

Be completely humble and gentle; be patient,
bearing with one another in love.
EPHESIANS 4:2

Born with Down syndrome, two-year-old Eliza Sankey has physical therapy, occupational therapy, speech therapy, and an educator who comes to the house. She also has six older brothers and sisters. "Her therapists say all the time she has her own therapy with her siblings," said Alana, Eliza's mom.

When Chad and Allison Shelley learned they were pregnant with their second child, Parker, their firstborn son Jackson had been recently diagnosed with autism, and his therapies left the Shelleys short on cash, time, and energy. Yet "Parker has been the greatest gift we could have ever given Jackson," said Allison. "No one teaches you social boundaries quite like a sibling."

Gillian Marchenko has watched her two oldest daughters lead the way in loving and prodding along Polly, who has Down syndrome and a stroke and seizure disorder. Polly, in turn, has nudged along her adopted sister, Evie, who has Down syndrome and autism, in her development. "Sisters are the best therapists in the world," wrote Gillian.[8]

The truth is, we all need "sibling therapy." We get that, in part, from other parents of children with special needs. Amanda Paragon, whose son also has a diagnosis on the autism spectrum, shared that while a group of children with ASD had therapy together, the parents "had our own therapy time where we could confide about our struggles, and how painful it is when well-meaning people would give us unsolicited parenting advice or say downright judgmental things about how out of control our children were." Sharing the journey—whether online or face-to-face—is therapeutic indeed!

As believers, we also get sibling therapy from our brothers and sisters in Christ as we prod each other along in our growth and maturity in Christ. We need each other.

Paul tells us, "We who are strong ought to bear with the failings of the weak and not to please ourselves. Each of us should please our neighbors for their good, to build them up" (Rom. 15:1–2). Some days you will be the strong one who is to build up a struggling friend. Other days, the roles will be reversed. When we build up our brothers and sisters in Christ, bolstering their faith, we bring encouragement to each other and glory to God (vv. 5–6).

Dozens of "one another" commands in the New Testament show us that sibling therapy is an integral aspect of being a child of God. Let's consider just some of them. We are to

- love one another (John 13:34);
- carry each other's burdens (Gal. 6:2);
- forgive each other (Eph. 4:32);
- speak to one another with psalms, hymns, and spiritual songs (Eph. 5:19);
- teach and admonish one another (Col. 3:16);
- encourage and build each other up (1 Thess. 5:11);
- spur one another on toward love and good deeds (Heb. 10:24); and
- pray for each other (James 5:16).

What a difference it would make if we consistently kept this list in mind as we interact with our families, our churches, with other friends who have kids with special needs—and with friends who don't. We need our pastors, small group leaders, and counselors. But we also need our brothers and sisters in Christ to show us by example how to walk in faith, to gently steer us back onto the path when we stumble, to help shoulder our burdens, and to cheer for our spiritual growth along the way.

"Above all, love each other deeply, because love covers over a multitude of sins. Offer hospitality to one another without grumbling. Each of you should use whatever gift you have received to serve others, as faithful stewards of God's grace in its various forms" (1 Peter 4:8–10).

Just as siblings are a priceless gift to our special children, brothers and sisters in Christ are treasures in our own lives. Whether for our children or ourselves, sibling therapy works!

Lord, thank you for my brothers and sisters in Christ! Open my eyes to opportunities to love and support them. Show me how to be a faithful steward of my gifts as I encourage my spiritual siblings. Above all, may we glorify you. In Jesus's name, amen.

DIGGING DEEPER
1. Whom can you encourage today? How?
2. Which families will you commit to praying for daily?
3. Which gift has God given you that you can use to serve your brothers and sisters?

INDISPENSABLE

Kimberly

There are many parts, but one body. The eye cannot say to
the hand, "I don't need you!" And the head cannot say to
the feet, "I don't need you!" On the contrary, those parts
of the body that seem to be weaker are indispensable.

1 CORINTHIANS 12:20-22

On any given Sunday, you can find my daughter Abbey giving
hugs, a high five, or saying hello to anyone and everyone. But
if you really want a treat, sit behind her during praise and worship.
You will see her with both hands raised high, and although she can't
speak, she sometimes vocalizes at the top of her lungs. She is a sight to
behold. People often come up to me in tears afterward to tell me how
much her worship has blessed them. She is a living example of Psalm
63:4. What would church be like without kids like Abbey? It would be
missing something beautiful, something meant to encourage the body
of Christ.

Paul wrote about this in his first letter to the Corinthians:

But God has put the body together, giving greater honor to
the parts that lacked it, so that there should be no division in

the body, but that its parts should have equal concern for each other. If one part suffers, every part suffers with it; if one part is honored, every part rejoices with it.

Now you are the body of Christ, and each one of you is a part of it. (1 Cor. 12:24–27)

The church needs our children to be a part of it because they have a role, a job to do. Maybe it is to teach compassion, to inspire heartfelt worship, to stretch us to be more flexible, or to open our minds to the needs of others. Whatever it is, each one of our children is *indispensable* (1 Cor. 12:22). Merriam-Webster defines the word as "not subject to being set aside or neglected . . . absolutely necessary: essential."[9]

Twenty-year-old Jake Lucas, who has autism, listened intently one Sunday as his pastor asked the congregation to hug someone in the spirit of Romans 16:16 before leaving the sanctuary. No one expected what happened next. "That's when the broken little toe led the foot, and the foot led the leg, and the leg led the body, and the weaker member became indispensable," wrote Jake's father, Greg. While most folks settled for awkward back-slaps and side-hugs, Jake bolted from his seat to bear hug an older gentleman clearly on his way out the door. The reluctant gentleman eventually melted into Jake's embrace as the congregation looked on. Jake then went from church member to church member with a hug for each. His genuine affection and joy quickly caught on as church members began to truly hug one another. "That Sunday started something new for Jake," wrote Greg, "and something new for the local body of Christ at Redemption Church—a sort of mini revival set afire by the unsuspecting, silent ember of one indispensable blazing heart."[10]

Kyle DeGroat has spent years as an usher and greeter for our church. While his Down syndrome makes it difficult for him to do some things, he is quick to give you a hug from behind while waiting for the offering plate to get back to him. His love and enthusiasm for every person who walks through the door are an example to us all. When he won a second-place medal for alpine skiing in the Special Olympics, the congregation erupted in celebration. He's indispensable. We need him.

Your child is indispensable too. When you bring him or her to church, you are bringing to the body of Christ a needed, treasured, and valuable member. What a beautiful thing. Your church is better off because your family is part of it.

> *Dear Lord, you are amazing. I am so touched by your heart for my child. Your love for those who are considered weak in this world is beyond what I could ever imagine. Thank you for creating us with different strengths and weaknesses so that, as one body, we can glorify you. In Jesus's name, amen.*

DIGGING DEEPER

1. What special qualities or gifts does your child have that might encourage other believers?
2. What has your child taught you about who God is?
3. List the ways having your child in church benefits other members of your church.

DEEP CAREGIVER LOVE

Kimberly

The LORD appeared to us in the past, saying:
"I have loved you with an everlasting love; I have
drawn you with unfailing kindness."
JEREMIAH 31:3

After nineteen years of caring for her daughter with severe autism, Wendy Hilton was tired. But when her daughter was hospitalized, God showed Wendy a profound picture of love. "I realized that my daughter, even though she can't express it with words, was always calmer when her daddy and I were close by than when the doctors and nurses were close by. I realized that, if her daddy and I were giving her medication, she took it (mostly) without incident. . . . She knew that we loved her and were there to take good care of her."

That's when God brought Romans 8:28 to Wendy's mind: "We know that in all things God works for the good of those who love him, who have been called according to his purpose." It was a powerful reminder.

"He loves and cares for me no matter whether I'm grateful or obedient or faithful to Him," Wendy wrote. "He allowed me to see my daughter as He sees me—helpless, not knowing the best way to take care of myself, not understanding at times what is going on around me or why or what to do about it. But just like my daughter was completely dependent on her daddy and me, if I will allow Him, God will comfort me, show me the right path, take care of me . . . just like my daughter trusts me to do for her."[11]

My daughter Abbey relies on me for every single aspect of her day in order to survive and thrive. Not only has she come to depend on my care, but because I provide that care, she has developed a great love for me. We are inseparable. I'm her best friend. She would choose me over a thousand others, probably, every single time. I would do anything for her, even give up my own life to protect her.

God the Father feels the same way about us. Ephesians 1:4–6 says, "He chose us in [Christ] before the creation of the world to be holy and blameless in his sight. In love he predestined us for adoption to sonship through Jesus Christ, in accordance with his pleasure and will—to the praise of his glorious grace, which he has freely given us in the One he loves." Like children welcomed into a family through the beauty of adoption, God has made us his sons and daughters.

Romans 8:38–39 talks about God's great caregiving love for us: "I am convinced that neither death nor life, neither angels nor demons, neither the present nor the future, nor any powers, neither height nor depth, nor anything else in all creation, will be able to separate us from the love of God that is in Christ Jesus our Lord."

Just as we would and will do anything for our children, God would and will do anything for us, even love us to the point of death. "He made himself nothing by taking the very nature of a servant, being made in human likeness. And being found in appearance as a man, he humbled himself by becoming obedient to death—even death on a cross!" (Phil. 2:7–8).

We can let ourselves feel safe in that kind of love. As much as you love your child, there is no deeper love than God's love for us. "Greater love has no one than this: to lay down one's life for one's friends" (John 15:13). Find rest in that love today.

Father, thank you for being my caregiver. Help me never to forget how deeply you love me and that nothing can separate me from your love. Thank you for giving me a real-life example of that in how I love my child. In Jesus's name, amen.

DIGGING DEEPER

1. Describe the love you feel toward your child.
2. How has that love increased as the result of being your child's caregiver?
3. What does it mean to you to have God as your caregiver?

SIX

Sunlit
Turning Toward the Son

You, LORD, keep my lamp burning;
my God turns my darkness into light.

PSALM 18:28

EYES WIDE OPEN

Jocelyn

I pray that the eyes of your heart may be enlightened in order
that you may know the hope to which he has called you.

EPHESIANS 1:18

"If we don't take the baby, you'll die, and so will she." Allie Powell reeled at the words. She was twenty-five weeks pregnant.

And then, suddenly, she wasn't.

Baby Grey weighed fifteen ounces when she was taken by C-section. Doctor reports swirled in Allie's ears: She has a fifty-fifty chance. She may be too tiny to intubate. There's a hole in her heart. She very likely has bleeding in the brain.

But Grey did tolerate intubation, the hole in her heart could be fixed with medication, and miraculously, there was no bleeding in the brain. Her eyes, however, remained fused shut when they should have opened within a few days. "Blind," the doctors predicted.

Allie's heart sank further with every passing day. "Open her eyes, Lord," she whispered, gazing at her fragile micro-preemie. "Please, just open her eyes."

A week passed. Then two. Then three. Hope faded, and darkness descended upon Allie's spirit as well.

So often we can't see what our heavenly Father is doing. Sometimes all we know is pain and darkness. It's isolating, disorienting—and misleading.

Just because we can't see doesn't mean there is nothing to see.

In Genesis 21, Sarah drove out her slave, Hagar, along with Ishmael, the baby Hagar had conceived by Abraham. When Hagar's supply of water was gone, she waited, sobbing, for young Ishmael to die.

But God, whom Hagar had earlier named El Roi, the "God who sees me" (Gen. 16:13), not only spoke to her but "opened her eyes and she saw a well of water. So she went and filled the skin with water and gave the boy a drink" (21:19). The well was there all along. She just couldn't see it until the Lord opened her eyes.

When Elisha's servant quaked in the face of the enemy, Elisha prayed, "'Open his eyes, Lord, so that he may see.' Then the Lord opened the servant's eyes, and he looked and saw the hills full of horses and chariots of fire all around Elisha" (2 Kings 6:17).

Jesus literally opened the eyes of the blind, and, just as miraculously, he can enlighten the eyes of our hearts today (Eph. 1:18). Perhaps his greatest demonstration of hope unseen took place on Calvary.

During the week leading up to Easter one year, Kathryn Sneed learned that her baby girl, who had stumped specialists almost since birth and had been on a feeding tube for months, had tested "border-line" for cystic fibrosis. That Holy Week, Kathryn wasn't feeling very holy.

But one quote stuck with her: "Easter Saturday: The eternal reminder that God is still at work even when He seems silent."

"So maybe we are just in that waiting period," Kathryn wrote on her blog.[1] "Maybe it's Easter Saturday and God is still working. Maybe there is a plan that is better than I could ever imagine." When we can't see God, it's not because he's disappeared.

Baby Grey's eyes did open on their own, and her vision is fine. At a year old and eleven pounds, she exhibits developmental delays, and at times, Allie struggles not to worry. "We need to keep our eyes on God and not on our own circumstances," she said. "I have to trust him."

May we all strive to keep our eyes wide open to his presence. But even more important, even if our eyes are closed as tightly as Grey's once were, may we remember that El Roi, the God who sees, is still there. And he is always at work.

God who sees, open my eyes to your presence. Help me trust that when I can't hear or see you at work, you're still working. You've got a plan, and you're in control. Thank you that I don't have to be! In Jesus's name, amen.

DIGGING DEEPER

1. How do you feel when you focus on your circumstances?
2. How does your attitude change when you shift your focus onto the character of God?
3. If you could see what God sees when he looks at your child, what would you see?

SECRET KEEPER

Kimberly

Rejoice always, pray continually, give thanks in all
circumstances; for this is God's will for you in Christ Jesus.
1 THESSALONIANS 5:16-18

While driving in the car one day, I asked my nine-year-old son
to tell me some things that he liked about having a sister with
disabilities. With great enthusiasm he shouted from the back seat,
"That's easy. She keeps every secret!" I couldn't stop laughing. It's true!
Sometimes having a nonverbal child has certain joys that no one else
can truly appreciate. Our boys will certainly experience some struggle
and hardship because of having a disabled sister, but they are sure to
experience just as many unexpected joys and blessings.

In a world that loves to vent online and in social media, it's easy
to get caught up in the negative things of this life. Philippians 4:8
reminds us where we should plant our thoughts: "Finally, brothers and
sisters, whatever is true, whatever is noble, whatever is right, whatever
is pure, whatever is lovely, whatever is admirable—if anything is excellent or praiseworthy—think about such things." We must ask ourselves
while we are reading, listening, or talking with others, "Is this truth?
Is it noble and right? Is it pure, lovely, and admirable? Is it excellent or

praiseworthy?" If it doesn't pass this litmus test, then we should move on quickly to something that does.

When we spend time with our minds fixed on the things of God, it changes our perspective on how we view the trials of this life. The life of Paul is a perfect example. His hardships were many. He shares them in detail in 2 Corinthians 11:23–27. He was imprisoned, flogged, beaten, stoned, and shipwrecked. His life was threatened at sea, in the country, in the city, and by bandits, Jews, Gentiles, and false believers. He adds, "I have labored and toiled and have often gone without sleep; I have known hunger and thirst and have often gone without food; I have been cold and naked" (v. 27).

The same Paul who has been through all of this also encourages the Thessalonians: "Rejoice always, pray continually, give thanks in all circumstances; for this is God's will for you in Christ Jesus" (1 Thess. 5:16–18). After all he had been through, Paul continues to go back to a life centered on the gospel for hope and strength in his weaknesses.

When our thought life and our spoken life don't match up with the things of God, we have to go back to Christ. He alone can transform our hearts and minds. Like David in Psalm 139:23–24, we can cry out, "Search me, God, and know my heart; test me and know my anxious thoughts. See if there is any offensive way in me, and lead me in the way everlasting."

When we are tempted to have a negative heart that sees only the demands of taking care of our children, may we open our minds to the good, the true, and the lovely instead. Just as my son rejoices that his nonverbal sister is a fantastic secret keeper, I pray that the rest of us can rejoice in what is pure, excellent, or praiseworthy.

Dear Lord, thank you for all the great joys and blessings you have given me because of my child. I know I don't always try to look for what is pure and true, so I ask you to continue to show me how to have a heart like yours. In Jesus's name, amen.

DIGGING DEEPER

1. What are some things you have grown to enjoy about having a child with disabilities?
2. What are specific characteristics of your child that you love?
3. How can you practice the art of giving thanks and dwelling on the things of God in your life?

UNKNOWN PROTECTIONS

Jocelyn

He will command his angels concerning you to guard
you in all your ways; they will lift you up in their hands,
so that you will not strike your foot against a stone.

PSALM 91:11-12

When Rebekah Benimoff's diabetic son has a seizure, she injects the emergency shot of insulin as quickly as possible. The minutes that follow, however, drag on like hours as the sugar stores in his body release to stop the seizing. In those moments, she protects him from falling off a bed or otherwise hurting himself. She strokes his head and whispers assurance even if it is only to his subconscious. "And this is what I have found that God does for us in the moment when we cannot stop and take a deep breath," she said. "He draws near, giving emergency assistance in many forms, even if we do not recognize it is the hand of God moving."

Jesus promised troubles in this life (John 16:33), and yet Psalm 91 paints a beautiful picture of God's protection for his faithful. These verses point to a divine presence that is unseen and perhaps even unnoticed. Verses 14–15 tell us: "'Because he loves me,' says the LORD, 'I will rescue him; I will protect him, for he acknowledges my name. He will call on me, and I will answer him; I will be with him in trouble, I will deliver him and honor him."

But what kind of protection is this, exactly? We may never know on this side of heaven, just as Tyler is not aware of his mother's protection during his seizures. Perhaps while we are unaware of God's presence at all, he is standing over us, shielding us from unknown dangers. Perhaps he is even weeping with us as Jesus wept alongside Lazarus's sisters when Lazarus was in the tomb (John 11:35). Perhaps he is standing just outside the grave, arms outstretched, waiting for us to come to him.

Rebekah sees it this way: "Through those he brings to help, through the touch of his hand in a kind word, and his feet in a meal delivered, he draws near. He is that comforting presence that keeps us protected in his hands until the chaos subsides. He protects us in ways we may not ever comprehend, but he is there, even when the presence feels very subconscious at the moment. He is stroking your spirit, whispering those quiet words of assurance: 'Come to me, draw near, and you will find help, hope, and healing.'"

It may be harder to recognize God's presence in moments of emergency or trauma or pain, but the Bible tells us he is with us through it all. "When you pass through the waters, I will be with you; and when you pass through the rivers, they will not sweep over you. When you walk through the fire, you will not be burned; the flames will not set you ablaze" (Isa. 43:2). He is even with us as we walk through the darkest valley (Ps. 23:4). He is truly our "ever-present help in trouble" (Ps. 46:1).

These days, Rebekah actively practices looking for and to the Lord's comforting presence in times of crisis, exhaustion, fear, and everyday stress. Like her, you may find it helpful to post Scriptures around the house as reminders. "When we invite him into those moments, he never fails to accept. He is always available, always timely, and always faithful."

Lord, thank you that even though I can't always see you, you are always with me. Help me look for you more often. Help me grasp your presence and your comfort, even when it comes in the form of other people's helping hands and encouraging words. In Jesus's name, amen.

DIGGING DEEPER

1. Looking back, when and how can you see God's hand working during a previous crisis?
2. What is one verse or passage you want to memorize to remind you of God's presence?
3. Name one way you've noticed God giving you emergency assistance.

FACING THE FUTURE

Kimberly

"I know the plans I have for you," declares the LORD,
"plans to prosper you and not to harm you, plans to
give you hope and a future."
JEREMIAH 29:11

Medical crisis leaves me spinning. Like a child on a merry-go-round, I'm fine at first, but after a while things get blurry and I start to feel sick. I get thrown off my balance pretty quickly when our daughter is facing a new challenge or even a common cold. Because let's face it, there is no such thing as a "common" cold for a child with disabilities. Everything can lead to something, and I never know what that something is going to be. There is so much uncertainty. I hold my breath when I see the phone number for my daughter's school show up on my caller ID. The slightest cough or cry jerks me out of bed in the middle of the night. It's during these times of uncertainty that I cling to promises like Jeremiah 29:11. When everything around me is a blur, I know that the Lord knows exactly what's going on, and what the outcome will be. He wants to give me *real* hope. Hope not in my circumstances but in his promises.

I appreciate the word *declare* in this passage of Scripture. The word can mean a number of things: to make known formally or officially; to state emphatically or authoritatively; to affirm; to reveal or make manifest, and more.[2] You almost expect to hear a trumpet call and someone with a deep resonating voice saying, "The King declares . . ." It's true: God is making his words in Jeremiah official. He's stating emphatically, with all the authority of the King of Kings, "I know the plans I have for you." There is a deep rest in that.

First Corinthians 2:9 says, "Things which eye has not seen and ear has not heard, and which have not entered the heart of man, all that God has prepared for those who love him" (NASB). I don't know about you, but I'm feeling better already! I have no idea what he has in store for me but he says it's beyond my imagination.

We read one book later in 2 Corinthians 4:16–18: "Therefore we do not lose heart. Though outwardly we are wasting away, yet inwardly we are being renewed day by day. For our light and momentary troubles are achieving for us an eternal glory that far outweighs them all. So we fix our eyes not on what is seen, but on what is unseen, since what is seen is temporary, but what is unseen is eternal." That's the key.

It's so hard to remember that life isn't always about the visible *right now*. Our right-now troubles are temporary, even when they seem chronic. Sometimes we may feel like we're wasting away. But when we hold on to these promises in Jeremiah and the letters to the Corinthians, we can experience hope.

Our spirits can wait out our circumstances. Until the final word is penned in God's great story of our lives, the plan is still unfolding. Our life has far more eternal significance than our daily routines. It is greater than the sum of everything that was and is yet to be. God promises it will be beyond our imagination.

Thank you, Jesus, for holding my life in your hands. I get discouraged sometimes by my struggles and routines, but I do believe you have great plans for me. Thank you for the promises in your Word

that help me to have hope in the future you have planned for me.
In Jesus's name, amen.

DIGGING DEEPER

1. Are you caught in a rut of going through the motions of your daily routines?

2. Reread 1 Corinthians 2:9 and 2 Corinthians 4:16–18. What do these Scriptures say to your heart in your situation right now?

3. What are some simple, practical things you can do to focus yourself on God's promises of a future and a hope?

CHILDREN OF GOD

Jocelyn

Those who are led by the Spirit of God are the children of
God. The Spirit you received does not make you slaves,
so that you live in fear again; rather, the Spirit you received
brought about your adoption to sonship. And by him we cry,
"Abba, Father." The Spirit himself testifies with our spirit
that we are God's children.

ROMANS 8:14-16

When Gillian and Sergei Marchenko adopted Evangeline from
Ukraine, they knew what to expect from her Down syndrome
to some degree, since their third daughter, Polly, was also born with it.
What they did not expect was Evangeline's autism.

The adjustment was difficult, to say the least. But eighteen months
later, it finally felt like Evie knew she was home. It used to be that when
Evie got hurt, she would seek her crib for comfort rather than Gillian.
Those days are over.

"Now she comes to me and puts her arms up for me to take her,"
wrote Gillian. Evie's cognitive development hadn't progressed much,
and she still mostly didn't communicate, but she did say Mama and
Papa, and she had grown to seek out Gillian when she was hurt. "Most

of the time when she wants me, I can't think of anything better than spending some time loving on my girl. . . . Our love is hard earned. But the reward is that much greater because of it."[3]

As believers, we too have been adopted. Though we were once "children of wrath" (Eph. 2:3 NASB), we are now children of God (Rom. 8:14), saved by grace. Just as the Marchenkos chose Evangeline before she loved them, so our heavenly Father chose us while we had absolutely nothing to offer him. "We love because he first loved us" (1 John 4:19). He loved us even while we were in rebellion against him, and he paid the ultimate price to bring us into his kingdom. "But God demonstrates his own love for us in this: While we were still sinners, Christ died for us" (Rom. 5:8).

Our adoption story doesn't end there, however. Being named a child of God is just the beginning. I've been a believer for many years, and yet sometimes, I still resemble little Evangeline during her first year and a half in the Marchenko family. Like her, I don't always seek God out throughout the day. When I get hurt, reaching out to God is not always the first thing I do, though it should be. And if we're honest with ourselves, do we spend enough time with him, not because we're in crisis but just for the sheer joy of being in his presence? Are we in the Word, eager to know what our Father has to say to us?

Just as the Marchenkos delight in hearing Evangeline, who is mostly nonverbal, say "Mama" and "Papa," the Lord loves hearing us call for him as well. In fact, Romans 8:15 says we get to call the Creator of the universe our *Abba* Father. *Abba* is an Aramaic word used as a term of tender endearment by a beloved child in an affectionate, dependent relationship with her father. It would be like calling God "Daddy" or "Papa." Jesus cried out to his *Abba* Father from the garden of Gethsemane (Mark 14:36), and we're told we have the right to use the same term of endearment as children of God as well!

"See what great love the Father has lavished on us, that we should be called children of God! And that is what we are!" (1 John 3:1). Even when we stray from spending time with him, his love for us never falters. Rejoice! Today, let's embrace our sonship and seek our Father. If we are hurt, let's go to him first. Let's pour out our hearts to him (Ps. 62:8) and believe that our *Abba* Father will take care of us.

> Abba *Father, thank you for adopting me as your child! Thank you for loving me enough to sacrifice your only begotten Son that I might enjoy sonship with you as well. Remind me to come to you for any and all reasons. Help me never to forget the incredible blessing that you chose me before I knew you. In Jesus's name, amen.*

DIGGING DEEPER

1. When you're hurt, to whom or what do you turn first?
2. What is one thing you should talk to the Lord about today?
3. How could you do a better job of seeking God throughout the day?

THE RIDE OF YOUR LIFE

Kimberly

The God who made the world and everything in it is the
Lord of heaven and earth and does not live in temples
built by human hands. And he is not served by human
hands, as if he needed anything. Rather, he himself
gives everyone life and breath and everything else.

ACTS 17:24-25

We were visiting our local state fair, and Abbey's little brother was
in line for a toddler-size roller coaster. When I didn't put her in
line with him, she started to cry and point toward the ride. My husband
assured me she would be fine with him and motioned her up. The line
of parents parted, and we awkwardly walked her up the flight of stairs
to get in line with her dad. When she got situated on the ride, she waved
frantically and started squealing at the top of her lungs. As it took off,
all the little toddlers were holding on, and there was my ten-year-old
disabled daughter with a hand up in the air laughing her head off. She
had the ride of her life!

Parenting children with special needs is definitely scary at times.
We were chosen to get in line for this specific ride. The good news is,
our Dad is waiting at the top and assuring us that he'll be riding with

us. In the book of Joshua we see the Lord asking Joshua to step up as the leader of God's people. Joshua would lead God's people across the Jordan to inherit the Promised Land. Jericho stood in his way. But the Lord spoke to Joshua, saying,

> Be strong and very courageous. Be careful to obey all the law my servant Moses gave you; do not turn from it to the right or to the left, that you may be successful wherever you go. Keep this Book of the Law always on your lips; meditate on it day and night, so that you may be careful to do everything written in it. Then you will be prosperous and successful. Have I not commanded you? Be strong and courageous. Do not be afraid; do not be discouraged, for the Lord your God will be with you wherever you go. (Josh. 1:7–9)

When we carefully and daily study God's Word, we are equipped with everything we need to move forward. We can take our place in line without fear or discouragement, because God is with us.

When we doubt we are able, we remember that God made the world and everything in it, and he doesn't rely on us to do his job (Acts 17:24–25). He gives us life and breath and everything else. Like Abbey, we can throw our hands up in full confidence that God has got our circumstances under control.

Not only so, but there is an endless supply of joy that comes from being the parents of our children. The lessons we learn about God, about how our child enriches our families and communities, about ourselves, and about the ways this journey strengthens our relationships; the ways our children change us into better people, and the enjoyment their personalities give us—these are just a few of the things that overflow into joy.

But there is even greater joy in walking with Christ. "You make known to me the path of life; you will fill me with joy in your presence, with eternal pleasures at your right hand" (Ps. 16:11). The path of life is found in relationship with Jesus Christ; in him, no matter where he takes us, we can be filled with the joy of his presence.

> *Lord God, your ways are beyond my ways. Thank you for promising me that not only are you trustworthy, but you will also give me everything I need in order to do what you've called me to do. I thank you for the joys that have come from getting to share this ride with you, and for the joys that are yet unknown. In Jesus's name, amen.*

DIGGING DEEPER

1. Where and when do you feel God's presence in your life?
2. Which area of your life do you need to trust God to take care of?
3. List some of the joys you have already experienced as a result of parenting your child.

SOVEREIGN MOMENTS

Kimberly

All these people were still living by faith when they died.
They did not receive the things promised; they only saw
them and welcomed them from a distance, admitting
that they were foreigners and strangers on earth.

HEBREWS 11:13

Some parents have beautiful stories to share about their children coming into the world. Mine is different. In fact, it's difficult for me to talk about Abbey's birth because the traumatic nature of her delivery resulted in her having lifelong multiple disabilities. In my obstetrician's notes on that day, he cited "poor maternal effort" as part of the failure to progress. He failed to mention that he was asleep in another room for almost the entire delivery. When he did come to check on my progress, I was so embarrassed by the position the nurses had put me in to push, I begged to lay back down. He slipped out of the room quickly, and my daughter's life started to slip from our hands. In a few short hours he would rush in to deliver, look at her vitals, and yell, "Now!" In the following minutes I would watch her being resuscitated. In the following days I would beg God for her life. Over the last fourteen years I have revisited that day in my mind more times than I can count. Was someone to blame? Was I?

When tragedy strikes, pain looks for someone to blame. I blamed myself for many years, and our friends and family blamed my doctor. But the truth is, God could have intervened at any moment and yet he chose not to. In time, I grew to find comfort in his sovereignty over those moments. In his infinite knowledge and authoritative power, he chose not to alter the events in my life, or Abbey's life—or your child's life. Isaiah 46:9–10 talks about his sovereignty: "Remember the former things, those of long ago; I am God, and there is no other; I am God, and there is none like me. I make known the end from the beginning, from ancient times, what is still to come. I say, 'My purpose will stand, and I will do all that I please.'"

Job understood this. As a faithful servant of God, he lost his family and fortune and endured extreme physical suffering. In Job 38, the Lord comes to speak to Job's pain at last. In Job 42:1–3 we read his response: "Then Job replied to the Lord: 'I know that you can do all things; no purpose of yours can be thwarted. You asked, "Who is this that obscures my plans without knowledge?" Surely I spoke of things I did not understand, things too wonderful for me to know.'"

Romans 8:28 assures us that while our circumstances may be difficult or even painful, he can use them for good: "We know that in all things God works for the good of those who love him, who have been called according to his purpose." While it can be difficult to hear those words when our child is suffering, the struggle doesn't make them any less true. Find strength in 2 Corinthians 4:17: "Our light and momentary troubles are achieving for us an eternal glory that far outweighs them all."

We also realize that the eternal glory these trials are achieving may not be seen or felt in this life. Hebrews chapter 11 is a long list of God's faithful servants. While imperfect, their faith in God led them to do amazing things for him. Though faithful in this life, many never realized the role they would play in God's redemption story (vv. 13, 39). Their reward was in heaven. We too can continue to live a life of faithfulness before our sovereign God. While we may not understand his ways, we can still choose to believe they are beyond ours and walk in faithfulness before him (Isa. 55:8).

At thirty-five weeks pregnant, my dear friend Allison woke up from a nap covered in blood. She was rushed into an emergency C-section for a second-degree placental abruption. It was my obstetrician who saved her life and her sweet baby's life. Mere men make mistakes in one moment and rise to do amazing things in the next. God is sovereign over them all.

Father, I trust you with my life. I believe you are God. I believe you are good. I believe you will work these hard circumstances together for my good, even if I don't see the fruit of my faith in this life. In Jesus's name, amen.

DIGGING DEEPER

1. Do you find comfort in the sovereignty of God in your life?
2. What situations are out of your control that you can entrust to God today?
3. Are there ways you have already seen God working for good in your life?

WHAT'S IN A NAME?

Jocelyn

> For to us a child is born, to us a son is given,
> and the government will be on his shoulders. And he will
> be called Wonderful Counselor, Mighty God,
> Everlasting Father, Prince of Peace.
> ISAIAH 9:6

Names are meaningful. We carefully choose the names of our children. The names of their diagnoses unlock the next steps for their treatments, medicines, and therapies. And the names of Jesus hold promise and comfort for all of us.

Allison and Chad Shelley were thrilled with the progress their autistic son was making at a new clinic. They were also almost destitute because of it. Since their employer's insurance didn't cover the necessary therapy, they purchased their own policy, which cost as much as their monthly mortgage payment. Though they lived a simple lifestyle, they still needed to borrow from both sets of parents. For a while they paid for groceries by selling their plasma. Then they learned they were pregnant.

"Those were some dark days," Allison said. "We were down to the dollar, month after month. We had to rely on the Lord and on each other."

Jesus, the Bread of Life (John 6:35), sustained them. Those of us with genuine financial strain can fill up on Jesus daily, even as we ask for our daily bread (Matt. 6:11).

As a military wife with four children, three of whom have been diagnosed with autism, Priscilla Rhoades often struggles with her husband's absences. Yet, "Many times when he's gone, that's when I draw closer to God," she said. "During our first deployment, I believe God gave me the Scripture that says, 'For your Maker is your husband' (Isa. 54:5 NKJV). I've had quite a few opportunities to draw on that."

Whether you are a military spouse, divorced, widowed, or a solo caregiver for another reason, you can rely on your heavenly Bridegroom. "To all of us, male and female, Christ offers himself as our provider and protector, the one who has forever pledged himself in faithfulness and love," wrote Ann Spangler in *Praying the Names of Jesus*.[4]

The doctors told Penny Clark that nothing was the matter with her son. Penny knew they were wrong. He had severe vomiting, diarrhea, and dehydration, and he screamed in pain. Penny prayed for direction as she hunted down information.

Finally, "My prayers were answered in a parent chat board. I shared my son's story, and a mom responded immediately. She told me about Food Protein-Induced Enterocolitis Syndrome, a type of food allergy affecting the gastrointestinal (GI) tract, told me where to search for a doctor, and how to get help."

Looking back, Penny can see how the Good Shepherd guided her search. When we recognize his voice, as sheep know their own shepherd, he leads us.

After mourning the passing of their eleven-year-old son from Sanfilippo syndrome, Sue and Hector Badeau experienced Good Friday in a whole new way. God knows what it's like to lose a son too. "He grieves with us, but he also rejoices with us that the resurrection is not only for Jesus, but for Adam too," said Sue.[5] As the Badeaus rejoiced in that truth, they remembered Psalm 30:5: "Weeping may stay for the night, but rejoicing comes in the morning."

Jesus, the bright Morning Star (Rev. 22:16), had led them into their morning after their long night of grief. In ancient times, the morning star was regarded as the herald of the new day. Jesus ushers in a dawn of hope and joy from which all darkness flees.

Jesus is our Bread of Life, Bridegroom, Good Shepherd, and Morning Star. He is our Wonderful Counselor, Mighty God, Everlasting Father, and Prince of Peace. Call on him by his names today.

Wonderful Counselor, bring me wisdom. Prince of Peace, still my anxious heart. Mighty God, show yourself, and work in my life and the life of my child. Thank you for being all that I need! In Jesus's name, amen.

DIGGING DEEPER

1. Why did you choose your child's name?
2. Which name of Jesus resonates most with you right now?
3. Did any of these names of Jesus surprise you? If so, which one, and why?

MEDICAL DEBT, SPIRITUAL DEBT

Kimberly

> Give us today our daily bread. And forgive us our debts,
> as we also have forgiven our debtors.
>
> MATTHEW 6:11-12

I can see myself with vivid clarity. I am sitting in the middle of the living room floor surrounded by a pile of paperwork. To my left is a tiny pile of medical bills I've paid; spread across the middle are the many I haven't paid; and in a pile on the right are those that need to be reviewed because they don't match what my insurance should have paid. I am literally surrounded by medical debt. Apparently my "toss it in a pile and pretend it isn't there" method of organization wasn't going to cut it, as the new bills coming in were all on pink or yellow paper with the word "COLLECTIONS" written across the top. We hit an all-time low when I was served with court papers over a bill that, in the end, wasn't even our responsibility to pay. I didn't even know where to begin.

We can feel the same way about our sin. When we fully realize the extent to which our sin offends God, we can stick our heads in the sand and just pretend it isn't there. But then it starts to pile up, and the consequences start to come in, completely overwhelming us. We don't know where to begin.

Dave Ramsey's Financial Peace University classes teach that one of the first things you need to do is compile a list of all your current debts. You have to acknowledge that they exist. First John 1:9 shows us that first step toward spiritual peace is also acknowledging that our sins exist. "If we confess our sins, he is faithful and just and will forgive us our sins and purify us from all unrighteousness." This is where the similarities between medical debt and spiritual debt end. There is no need to snowball the list, to make phone calls and payment plans; there is no need to pay back one single thing. Our God is not a collection agent waiting to receive his due.

Romans 5:6–8 lays out his payment plan: "You see, at just the right time, when we were still powerless, Christ died for the ungodly. Very rarely will anyone die for a righteous person, though for a good person someone might possibly dare to die. But God demonstrates his own love for us in this: While we were still sinners, Christ died for us." His death reconciled us to a holy God (v. 10). Our account has been paid in full!

When we acknowledge our sin before God; trust in the blood his Son, Jesus, shed on the cross to save us from that sin; and turn our life over to him, then we are spiritually free, unshackled from the debt that once held us (see John 8:31–36). Yet while that debt has been paid and we are forever free of the sin that separated us from eternity with God, we will still continue to sin. When we snap at our spouse, when our pride keeps us from saying we're sorry to our children, when we tell a lie or gossip . . . his sacrifice on the cross continues to be enough to free us from that sin when we confess it.

As we walk with him, Christ forgives our repentant hearts and gives us everything we need to overcome. First Corinthians 10:13 encourages us that "no temptation has overtaken you except what is common to mankind. And God is faithful; he will not let you be tempted beyond what you can bear. But when you are tempted, he will also provide a way out so that you can endure it." Praise God, he is enough!

*Thank you, Lord, for canceling all my debts to you, for paying
them in full with the blood of your Son. Help me to live in the
freedom that comes from believing in your Son. In Jesus's name,
amen.*

Digging Deeper

1. How do you manage your medical debt? Could you benefit from seeking help?
2. What does this "paid in full" zero balance statement over your spiritual life mean to you?
3. In what areas of your life do you want to seek true spiritual freedom?

HEAVENLY DWELLING

Kimberly

We know that if the earthly tent we live in is destroyed,
we have a building from God, an eternal house in heaven,
not built by human hands. Meanwhile we groan, longing
to be clothed instead with our heavenly dwelling.

2 CORINTHIANS 5:1-2

When Abbey was learning to walk, she had a difficult time getting to sleep at night after a long day of therapy. I wondered if her legs hurt, so I would bring in some lotion and gently massage her legs to help her relax. She wouldn't always let me do this, but occasionally it seemed to give her great comfort. One night I sat over her and started to tell her about heaven. I told her that in heaven her legs would never hurt, that she would be able to talk, run, jump, and do anything she wanted to do. She looked me straight in the eyes—not an easy task for her—and then reached both hands up to gently grab my face. She pulled my head down so that our foreheads were touching, and we stayed this way for a long time. I started to cry and she wrapped me up in a hug. She understood. She has no words, but she understood every one of mine.

Abbey was created as a gift and is exactly who she was meant to be. All of Psalm 139 speaks to me, but especially verses 13–14: "You created my inmost being; you knit me together in my mother's womb. I praise you because I am fearfully and wonderfully made; your works are wonderful, I know that full well."

Our children were fearfully and wonderfully made. God knew their frames, he knit their bodies, he created them. Their earthly bodies have limitations, but praise God, it won't always be that way.

For our children with disabled minds and bodies, heaven holds the hope of bodies free of struggle and pain.

> For this perishable body must put on the imperishable, and this mortal body must put on immortality. When the perishable puts on the imperishable, and the mortal puts on immortality, then shall come to pass the saying that is written:
> "Death is swallowed up in victory."
> "O death, where is your victory?
> O death, where is your sting?" (1 Cor. 15:53–55 ESV)

Realizing that this temporary tent will be exchanged for a heavenly dwelling can make the unbearable bearable. Why do we long for this exchange? Second Corinthians 5:3–5 tells us: "Because when we are clothed, we will not be found naked. For while we are in this tent, we groan and are burdened, because we do not wish to be unclothed but to be clothed instead with our heavenly dwelling, so that what is mortal may be swallowed up by life. Now the one who has fashioned us for this very purpose is God, who has given us the Spirit as a deposit, guaranteeing what is to come." This guarantee can give us the strength to endure medical crises; it provides a reason to hope and comfort during the trials that come as a result of our child's earthly limitations.

While we go to doctors, control medications, and rub legs at night, Scripture is the lifeline that brings hope into dark moments. After a hard day with his son, Greg Lucas whispers Scripture to his son Jake and to himself. Scriptures like Philippians 3:20–21: "Our citizenship is in heaven. And we eagerly await a Savior from there, the Lord Jesus Christ, who, by the power that enables him to bring everything under his control, will transform our lowly bodies so that they will be like his glorious body."

In the book of Isaiah, we read prophecy about the coming of Christ and the wonders he will perform: "Then will the eyes of the blind be opened and the ears of the deaf unstopped. Then will the lame leap like a deer, and the mute tongue shout for joy. Water will gush forth in the wilderness and streams in the desert" (35:5–6). Such wonders are a glimpse into eternity and a vessel of hope for those who believe.

Father, thank you for the promise of glorious heavenly bodies. When I see my child struggling, I look forward to seeing him or her whole in you. In Jesus's name, amen.

DIGGING DEEPER
1. Read Psalm 139. How do these verses encourage you?
2. What limitations will your child be free of in heaven?
3. How can the promise of a heavenly body bring you hope today?

SEVEN

Pruned
When Pain Produces Fruit

He cuts off every branch in me that bears no fruit,
while every branch that does bear fruit he prunes
so that it will be even more fruitful.

JOHN 15:2

GLORIOUSLY DEPENDENT

Jocelyn

I am the vine; you are the branches. If you remain in me
and I in you, you will bear much fruit; apart from me
you can do nothing.

JOHN 15:5

Leslie Jurado winced. In this new phase of her daughter Izzy's Sanfilippo syndrome, Izzy physically hurt Leslie multiple times a day.
"She was too hyper and manic for me to even enjoy a cuddle," said
Leslie. "I wanted to be with her so badly, but her cognitive decline (de-
mentia) left her confused and agitated."

It was a desperate, isolating time for the Jurados. They survived
by practicing grace for their daughter and accepting God's grace for
their own perceived shortcomings as her parents. "During this period I
began to better understand God's love and grace for his children. Being
rejected and hurt by us, only to love us more with each passing day."

When Izzy had been diagnosed with the terminal disease at the
age of three, Leslie had flailed against God exactly the way Izzy railed
against her own parents during the wild years. "I drifted back and forth
between denial, bartering, and loads of anger. 'This is not fair, God! I
was going to raise her to serve you. How could you give her to me just

to watch her suffer and then take her away? Why did you give her to me to fall in love with and then rip my heart out with this fate?'"

Just as Leslie longed to hold Izzy close despite her daughter's aggression, God longs to be up close and personal with you, his beloved child, even if you're kicking, screaming, or spitting at him. We can be angry with him, and he won't turn his back on us. We can lash out at him, and he won't walk away. He can handle our fury and our sorrow. God will still be there when we find ourselves utterly exhausted.

After Leslie's initial shock and outrage over Izzy's diagnosis, she decided, "I could not dishonor her life and her suffering by not letting it change me. Anxieties that had plagued me prior to this diagnosis now seemed ridiculous. My daughter had gifted me with perspective."

In Izzy's current stage of Sanfilippo, she presents as a child with quadriplegic cerebral palsy. "She has endured eight years of intractable epilepsy and now struggles daily with uncontrollable, involuntary movements. Now that she is completely dependent, I feel that I am able to 'wash the feet of Jesus' in my care for her."

Loving unconditionally is a supernatural feat. Yet that's exactly what we're told to do in John 15:12–13: "My command is this: Love each other as I have loved you. Greater love has no one than this: to lay down one's life for one's friends." How can we lay down our lives, dying to self, day after day, night after night?

Only by tapping into his power. Jesus is the Vine; we are the branches. Only when we are connected to him—our very source of life—can we bear fruit. The apostle Paul wrote, "He said to me, 'My grace is sufficient for you, for my power is made perfect in weakness.' . . . For when I am weak, then I am strong" (2 Cor. 12:9–10).

The same is true for each of us. When we are weak, we can be strong through Christ. "Friends, God purifies our hearts in the fire if we allow him to," said Leslie. "He can show us through our special children that struggles and suffering make us gloriously dependent on him."

Lord, purify my heart. When I am angry and screaming at you, thank you for not turning away. When I'm weak, give me your strength. Help me depend on you as the branches depend on the vine. In Jesus's name, amen.

DIGGING DEEPER

1. Do you feel angry or hurt right now? If so, what is the main reason?
2. How do you see yourself as the presence of God in your child's life? In other words, what do you do for your child that is similar to what God does for us?
3. What is your greatest weakness for which you need God's help?

HE HATES BEING CLEANED

Jocelyn

This is love: not that we loved God, but that he loved us and
sent his Son as an atoning sacrifice for our sins. . . .
We love because he first loved us.

1 JOHN 4:10, 19

For Greg Lucas, every day begins the same way: with a jolting wake-fulness that beats the alarm, a fervent prayer for grace and strength, and a rush of adrenaline for the task ahead. It is time to clean Jake.

Greg's grown son violently resists the routine that makes him clean again. Not only does Jake have autism, OCD, and cerebral palsy, but he also has sensory integration disorder; the process and state of undress are a misery to him. The combination of having his backside wiped after his diaper is removed and the sound of the running bathwater amplifies his thrashing protests.

"It's not that Jake likes being dirty," Greg wrote in *Wrestling with an Angel*. "He just hates being cleaned."[1]

Greg's wife, Kim, provides necessary backup. One parent holds him in the tub while the other scrubs filth from his skin and hair, and from under his fingernails. After Jake is dried and dressed, Greg pins him down to brush his teeth while singing a soothing song. All the while,

Greg might be hit, kicked, clawed, or spit upon. By the end, he often feels dejected, hurt, and emotionally drained. "In desperation, I find myself restraining his struggles by wrapping him in my arms against his will and gently whispering, 'I love you—no matter what.'"[2]

The only way Greg has been able to continue loving his son, who seems incapable of returning affection, has been to understand the picture of God's unconditional love for his children.

"Much like my son, I have been disabled all my life," shared Greg. "My disability affects everything I am and everything I do. Scripture diagnoses this disability as a sin nature. It causes me to reject love and embrace fear, and makes me strangely satisfied to lie in my own filth. It's not that I like being dirty. I just hate being cleaned."[3]

But God is relentless in his love for his children. He is patient, gracious, compassionate—but he also wages war against our natural inclination to sin. As the apostle Paul wrote,

> In my inner being I delight in God's law; but I see another law at work in me, waging war against the law of my mind and making me a prisoner of the law of sin at work within me. . . . Thanks be to God, who delivers me through Jesus Christ our Lord!
>
> So then, I myself in my mind am a slave to God's law, but in my sinful nature a slave to the law of sin. (Rom. 7:22–23, 25)

We know the Lord loves us, but many of us struggle to understand how a loving, all-powerful God could allow—or even bring—such suffering into our lives. Perhaps you can relate to Greg, whose trials and weariness, rather than prompting him to run to the light, often drive him into the darkness instead. "By nature, I resist the One who ultimately has designed all these difficult conditions for my good and for His glory."[4]

In this Greg sees a picture of his own relationship with Jake. It's a reminder that the love exhibited on the cross overpowers our rebellion and scrubs us clean. God loves his children even when we are stained with sin, but he loves us too much to allow us to stay that way.

Lord, I confess I don't know how you're planning to bring about my good and your glory through every trial that comes to my family. But please make me hunger and thirst after righteousness. Let me not be content with my own sin. Cleanse me. In Jesus's name, amen.

DIGGING DEEPER

1. When you are weary, where do you tend to turn?
2. What is one habit or sin from which you need to be cleansed?
3. When you picture Jesus wrapping his arms around you, even though you have fought against him, how do you feel?

CAN WE HAVE A BETTER MARRIAGE?

Kimberly

Follow God's example, therefore, as dearly loved children
and walk in the way of love, just as Christ loved us and gave
himself up for us as a fragrant offering and sacrifice to God.
EPHESIANS 5:1-2

The radio was playing songs that made me think about God, and I didn't want to think about God because I wanted to think about how much I couldn't stand my husband instead. The Christian music filling my car reminded me of how far away from God my heart truly was. The Holy Spirit was begging me to lay down my anger, to practice the art of confession, to come back to Christ, and worst of all, to forgive.

Early in our marriage, the care of our child with disabilities began to consume my life, and the fear of it pushed my husband to stay at work rather than come home. Our marriage was starting to crumble. We needed Christ to change our lives and our marriage if we were going to make it as a couple.

In her book *How to Act Right When Your Spouse Acts Wrong*, Leslie Vernick discusses how God uses marriage to make us more like himself.[5] She explains how a marriage sometimes reveals the worst in us, and as it does, it gives us the opportunity to pursue holiness. Parenting a child with special needs can also show us these things about ourselves. Barb Dittrich shared, "It turns out that the journey of completely immersing myself in parenthood, with three children who each battle some sort of complex diagnosis, has been a two-decade-long lesson in dying to self. This has transformed my character as I separate from so much of my wretchedness, embracing the opportunity to look more like Jesus."[6] The combination of marriage and parenting a child with special needs is full of these revelations about our sinful nature. Each is an opportunity to ask God to make us more like himself.

Marital healing begins with searching our own hearts and confessing our sins to each other. "Examine yourselves to see whether you are in the faith; test yourselves. Do you not realize that Christ Jesus is in you—unless, of course, you fail the test?" (2 Cor. 13:5). James 5:16 tells us, "Therefore confess your sins to each other and pray for each other so that you may be healed. The prayer of a righteous person is powerful and effective."

As we each confess our sins to each other, we are given the chance to choose forgiveness over anger. Ephesians 4:31–32 is a guideline for what this looks like. "Get rid of all bitterness, rage and anger, brawling and slander, along with every form of malice. Be kind and compassionate to one another, forgiving each other, just as in Christ God forgave you." To choose not to forgive has serious implications. Matthew 6:15 offers a stern warning: "But if you do not forgive others their sins, your Father will not forgive your sins."

If we go through the steps of examining our hearts, confessing our sins, and seeking and offering forgiveness, then we can start to love the way that Christ has loved us. Romans 12:9–10 says, "Love must be sincere. Hate what is evil; cling to what is good. Be devoted to one another in love. Honor one another above yourselves."

Because of Christ, forgiveness, hard work, and prayer, Ryan and I have just celebrated our sixteenth wedding anniversary. Today we enjoy a deeper love and commitment to Christ and to each other than I ever thought possible.

Father, give me a heart like yours for my spouse. Show me the areas of our marriage where I need to change. Help me to love the way you love and forgive the way you forgive. Restore us, Lord, so our marriage is a better reflection of Christ and his bride, the church. In Jesus's name, amen.

Digging Deeper

1. Have you experienced marital strain because of the demands of caring for your child?
2. What changes can you make in your marriage to get back on track?
3. In what areas of your marriage do you need to trust God to work and heal?

PRIDE KILLER

Jocelyn

All of you, clothe yourselves with humility toward one
another, because, "God opposes the proud but shows favor
to the humble."
1 PETER 5:5

By his own admission, Greg Lucas is a prideful person. And, he says, his son, Jake, is a "pride killer."

When Jake was six years old, the Lucas family visited a large church in Louisville, Kentucky. Greg assumed the church wouldn't know how to handle his disabled son, typical of his attitude upon entering any church. "I assume that this will be another bad experience, making it impossible for me to focus on worship," he shares in his book *Wrestling with an Angel*. "This is one of the ugliest forms of pride in my life. The truth is, usually the only obstacle barricading my heart from true worship is my own self-centered arrogance."[7]

On this particular Sunday, fifteen minutes into the sermon, no one from the preschool class had come for Greg or his wife, Kim, so he began to relax.

Too soon. Apparently, Jake's leg braces had not prevented him from sneaking into the choir loft behind the pastor. All eyes were on him and the children's ministry worker, who was now chasing him on hands and knees in full view of the eight hundred–strong congregation. His former arrogance completely humbled by Jake's theatrics, Greg made the long walk down the aisle to the altar and claimed his son, to the rumbling chuckles of the crowd.

Other experiences did not end with smiles. Losing bowel control in the bleachers at a ballgame scattered a disgusted crowd and embarrassed Jake so thoroughly he began biting himself, screaming and kicking, until Greg threw his teenaged son over his shoulder and carried him away.

"Sometimes the process of humility is just plain humiliating," Greg wrote. "Society perceives humiliation as an ultimate failure to be avoided at all costs, but of course, God can use it for our ultimate success. He accomplishes meekness by crushing our pride in order to lavish us with the gift of true Christlike humility. And it is here, as we find ourselves covered in the stench of our pride, that the aroma of grace smells the sweetest."[8]

Humility is nonnegotiable in a Christ-follower, and yet pride is one of the most difficult sins to ferret out of our hearts. We can even be proud of how "humble" we are! But the Bible is rife with warning. Pride brings disgrace and downfall (Prov. 18:12). Humility brings wisdom (11:2), riches, honor, and life (22:4). Over and over in the New Testament, we are told of the gentleness and humility of Christ and exhorted to be like him.

Throughout the Bible, God uses the humble to display his own strength. Moses had a stutter and didn't want the job of leader, but he led God's people out of Egypt through the power of I Am. With only a sling and a stone, David, the young shepherd boy, slayed a giant who caused terror in everyone else. Sarah gave birth to a nation when she was well beyond her childbearing years. Even Rahab the prostitute was in the lineage of Christ. The King of Kings "made himself nothing by taking the very nature of a servant, being made in human likeness. And being found in appearance as a man, he humbled himself by becoming obedient to death—even death on a cross!" (Phil. 2:7–8).

"When humility comes in and exposes my self-focus," wrote Greg, "I want to be able to see it for what it is: a loving gift from the grace of God."[9]

> *Lord, search my heart and show me where my pride is. Help me clothe myself with humility. Help me see humbling experiences as a gift from you, not something to be avoided. Remind me daily of Jesus's ultimate example of humility, and help me become more like him. In Jesus's name, amen.*

Digging Deeper

1. When was the last time you were humbled? What happened?
2. When have you felt humiliated?
3. The next time something similar happens, how will you try to respond?

BROKENNESS

Jocelyn

My sacrifice, O God, is a broken spirit; a broken and
contrite heart you, God, will not despise.

PSALM 51:17

When Lon Solomon became the senior pastor of McLean Bible
Church, located just outside Washington, D.C., he dreamed it
would become a large, influential church. The dream wasn't bad. His
motives were.

One woman in his congregation informed him of his arrogance,
rebuked him for glorifying himself instead of Christ, and called his sins
hindrances to God working in his life and in the church.

Secretly, Lon wondered if she was on to something. He'd been
working hard at his job, but he knew that what he really needed was a
powerful movement of the Holy Spirit in his life. So he prayed to that
end, not realizing then that what he was asking for was brokenness.

And oh, did God break him. In 1992, his daughter was born.
Hundreds of seizures a month damaged Jill's brain, and Lon and his
wife, Brenda, were slipping into the deepest, darkest despair they'd ever
known.

"God used this pain and helplessness to do to me what he did to

Moses in the forty years between Exodus 1 and 2," wrote Lon. "He used it to strip away all my self-resourcefulness, self-wisdom, and self-sufficiency. He used it to shatter my self-will, my fleshly self-reliance, and my self-assurance. Success could never have refined me like this—and God knew it. . . . God used Jill's disability to bring me to the end of myself."[10]

It's at the end of ourselves that we meet with God more closely than ever before—even if that closeness begins with a wrestling match, as it did when Jacob wrestled all night with God, begging for blessing (Gen. 32:24–26). Moses was broken, and Exodus 33:11 tells us, "The LORD would speak to Moses face to face, as one speaks to a friend."

Not many of us would ask God to break us. But when he does, he builds us up again to more closely resemble his Son. We are more compassionate, meek, and forgiving. "I have realized, you have to be broken in order to be fixed properly," Anne-Marie Wurzel wrote as she approached the anniversary of her daughter's metabolic crisis. "God is taking my brokenness and using it to help me be the type of mom and wife I need to be, and in order for that to come through, I need to be refined. God gave us Reagan to draw us, and others, closer to him. Because of Reagan, I feel like I understand God more. . . . And I feel like our whole family is under God's wing. The thing[s] that matters most in this life are the decisions you make for eternity."[11]

Since Lon was broken, McLean Bible Church has grown and become one of the leading churches in America in ministering to people with disabilities, especially children. "None of this would have happened had it not been for God blessing us with Jill."[12]

That which breaks us can also become a blessing. It may take years, but God does not waste the pain.

Lord, being broken hurts. My flesh asks this cup to be taken from me, but if my family must suffer, please use it. Bring beauty from ashes. My heart echoes the psalmist: "Make us glad for as many days as you have afflicted us, for as many years as we have seen trouble" [Ps. 90:15]. In Jesus's name, amen.

Digging Deeper

1. Was there a specific time or period when you felt that God broke you? If so, describe that experience.
2. How have you changed since then?
3. In what ways is God using you now that could not have happened before you were broken?

KEEP WALKING

Kimberly

In your unfailing love you will lead the people
you have redeemed. In your strength you will guide them
to your holy dwelling.

EXODUS 15:13

The large brown box arrived and sat on our living room floor. My husband, Ryan, and I sat staring at it; neither of us had the courage to open it. Inside was the first of many pieces of medical equipment that would arrive to help our daughter, Abbey, gain physical strength and independence. Though she was three years old, we were still carrying her everywhere. Doctors had told us she would likely never walk alone. We cried as Ryan put the pint-size walker together and the reality of her disabilities began sinking in. We were afraid, and honestly, we didn't want to go down this path.

The Israelites knew what it was like to be afraid and unwilling to continue on the path to which God had called them. As they left Egypt, they turned to see Pharaoh and his great army chasing after them. Stuck between Pharaoh and the sea, they said, "It would have been better for us to serve the Egyptians than to die in the desert!" (Exod. 14:12). But God parted the sea for the Israelites to walk through safely, destroying

Pharaoh's army as Moses and the people watched from the opposite shore. In an effortless stroke across the waters, God displayed his glory as well as the depth of his love, might, and faithfulness to his people. Fear of moving forward could have kept the Israelites from seeing God at work.

Fear almost kept us from seeing God at work too. When we first tried to get Abbey to use the walker, she would cry and reach for us. We had to ignore her reaching arms and make a game out of using it. We even ran a jump rope through the bars to slowly pull her along if she wouldn't go. If the walker started to move, she had to move with it or she would fall. We took the walker and the jump rope everywhere. People stared at us as we made her use it; some even suggested that what we were doing was cruel. Sometimes we wondered whether we were doing the right thing, but we knew in our hearts that if she could learn to walk, we were giving her the gift of independence and health. Almost three years later, Abbey began to refuse to use the walker and walked by herself.

Sometimes in our walk with Christ, we don't want to move forward because what he's asking us to do is difficult. But he promises to never leave us or forsake us (Deut. 31:6; Heb. 13:5). As the journey with him becomes difficult, we have to remember that he's trying to give us all that we need to live a life that is strong in him. There are oppositions along the way, but his Word tells us, "Consider it pure joy, my brothers and sisters, whenever you face trials of many kinds, because you know that the testing of your faith produces perseverance. Let perseverance finish its work so that you may be mature and complete, not lacking anything" (James 1:2–4). Later in verse 12 we read, "Blessed is the one who perseveres under trial because, having stood the test, that person will receive the crown of life that the Lord has promised to those who love him."

It can be a scary and difficult path between the shores of this life and the next. But if we trust Christ to show himself strong, and keep walking with him, we will be amazed when we reach the other side.

Lord, I ask you to give me the courage to keep walking with you, even when it hurts, because I know you're working in my life to give me spiritual maturity and health. You are for me, not against me, and I praise you for your faithfulness. In Jesus's name, amen.

DIGGING DEEPER
1. What struggles in your life are you finding it difficult to get through right now?
2. How do you see God working in your circumstances?
3. What are some lessons you have learned through past difficulty that you can now draw on to keep walking with him?

THE JOY OF SURRENDER

Jocelyn

Consider it pure joy, my brothers and sisters,
whenever you face trials of many kinds, because you know
that the testing of your faith produces perseverance.
Let perseverance finish its work so that you may be
mature and complete, not lacking anything.

JAMES 1:2-4

It took more than a year for Amanda Paragon to accept her son's diagnosis of autism spectrum disorder. Once she did, however, it changed everything.

"Surrendering to the validity of his diagnosis set me free to finally embrace this particular trial," she said. "My pride, foolishness, and misconceptions came to light as I commiserated with other moms during our sons' group therapy sessions. . . . And as my trials kept coming, I found that God (in his goodness and faithfulness) answered my prayers to make me a better mom—I found myself reacting to my son with more love and patience."

Surrendering to God's plan for our lives, including the special challenges our children have, is a prerequisite for joy and peace—and for God to fully use us for his glory. The Bible abounds with examples.

Abraham surrendered to God's command to lay his son Isaac on the altar. Hannah surrendered her long-awaited son, Samuel, back to God's service. Though Job questioned God's purpose, he still surrendered to his afflictions. Mary surrendered to the angel's news of Jesus's conception and birth, though she was surely reeling and confused. Even Jesus surrendered to the crucifixion, though he was "overwhelmed with sorrow to the point of death" (Matt. 26:38).

In her book *Surrender*, Nancy Leigh DeMoss wrote that God asks us to sign a blank contract for our life and let him fill in all the details afterward:

> "Why? Because I am God; because I have bought you; because I am trustworthy; because you know how much I love you; because you live for My glory and not your own independent, self-promoting pleasure."
>
> [When signing that blank paper] we cannot lose, because He is a God who can be completely trusted. If we will let Him, God will fill in the details of our lives with His incomparable wisdom and sovereign plan, written in the indelible ink of His covenant faithfulness and love.[13]

Notice that the promise in surrender is not a life of ease or happiness. We aren't even guaranteed to understand all the details of the plan as they unfold. When we surrender to God's will, we submit to his sovereignty, wisdom, faithfulness, and love. We also agree that the ultimate goal is God's glory alone.

When we are surrendered, we can consider trials pure joy for the fruit they produce (James 1:2–4). Since Amanda has surrendered to the path God established for her family, God has molded her more into his likeness. "I am now at a place where I can wholeheartedly say that I am a better mom, person, and most importantly follower of Jesus because we have been given the opportunity to live as parents to a beautiful son who is diagnosed with ASD," she said. "While I have not become the picture of patience by any means, I do hold on to that hope from James chapter one that as I count it all joy, God will continue to mold me in his perfect image to the point where I am complete and lack nothing."

For the believer, surrendering to Christ means victory.

Lord, it's hard for me to surrender to a future I don't know. But I do know you, and you are trustworthy. You are good. And I want you to use my life and my family for your glory. Help me submit to you on a daily basis—hourly, if need be. In Jesus's name, amen.

DIGGING DEEPER

1. What are you having a hard time accepting right now?
2. List three things you know for sure about God.
3. Think of a time you've surrendered something to God in the past. How did God prove his faithfulness?

DON'T PANIC!

Kimberly

Do not be anxious about anything, but in everything
by prayer and supplication with thanksgiving let your
requests be made known to God. And the peace of
God, which surpasses all understanding, will guard
your hearts and your minds in Christ Jesus.
PHILIPPIANS 4:6–7 (ESV)

Nights are difficult for me sometimes. I fall into bed exhausted, craving a moment of silence and solitude. Then when it comes, I find myself staring into the darkness and worrying about things concerning my daughter, all of which are serious. One night I actually felt my chest getting tighter and had difficulty breathing. What started out as a little worrying turned into a full-blown panic attack. I didn't even know what a panic attack was. It was terrifying! In the minutes that followed, as my husband helped me to calm down, I was able to see for the first time why the Lord tells us not to be anxious.

Anxiety is not uncommon; it is a typical response to extreme circumstances. But if not quelled, it reaches deep into our souls with a heaviness that can quickly be all-consuming. I struggle with it before the Lord regularly. I am comforted, however, by the reminder in Philippians 4:6 to present my requests to God. In the middle of anxious thoughts, we can settle our minds as we begin to pour out our hearts before the throne of grace. God cares very much about the things that concern his people. James 4:8 tells us to draw near to God with the assurance that he will draw near to us.

Philippians 4:6 also calls us to an attitude of thanksgiving as the perfect antidote to anxiety. How quickly the racing thoughts begin to disappear when we start to recount God's goodness. When we thank him for his faithfulness in the past and remember that his mercies are new every morning, we find ourselves in an attitude of praise. In times of worry and anxiety, we have by our side the Prince of Peace, the Great Counselor, Almighty God, our *Abba* Father. His names alone are often enough to calm my troubled spirit. When we really think of all that Christ has done for us, thanksgiving isn't difficult to come by.

The psalmist took the same approach to calm his spirit in Psalm 77. Early on he says, "I am so troubled that I cannot speak" (v. 4 ESV). But by verses 11 and 12 he's singing a different tune: "I will remember the deeds of the LORD; yes, I will remember your wonders of old. I will ponder all your work, and meditate on your mighty deeds."

A beautiful thing happens when we trade anxiety for prayer and thanksgiving. God's peace, that surpasses understanding, waits for us on the other side. There is no need to stay awake and let our minds go to dark places. If we can remember that with prayer and thanksgiving we can present ourselves and our worries to God, then the promise of his supernatural peace is ours to claim.

Note: If you suffer from regular or debilitating anxiety or from medically related traumatic stress (see "Crushed Spirit," p. 127), please seek help from a trusted counselor.

Jesus, when I feel anxious, help me pour out my heart to you. I know you hear me, and I know you love me. Thank you, Lord, for

working in my life and my circumstances. Help me know you are
near. In Jesus's name, amen.

DIGGING DEEPER

1. When do you seem to be most vulnerable to anxiety?
2. What are some things you can do—or avoid doing—to make
   yourself less vulnerable to panic?
3. The next time you struggle with anxiety, what do you hope to
   remember?

RESCUED HEARTS

Jocelyn

Search me, God, and know my heart; test me and know my
anxious thoughts. See if there is any offensive way in me,
and lead me in the way everlasting.

PSALM 139:23-24

R aising a child with special needs inevitably yields a different perspective on life. Things that used to matter pale in comparison to
what is really important. Rob Wurzel describes being a father to his
daughter, who suffered a metabolic crisis that caused brain damage, as
"a jailbreak for my heart." He explains on his blog:

It has been a violent process of ripping away "little indulgences" that my heart had learned to live on. . . . Sports,
TV, video games, home projects, movies, it was all cut away
like a skilled surgeon was carving out the cancerous parts
that plagued my heart. I'm amazed at how little I miss these
things as they are now simply a "treat," as they should be. . . .
Becoming a father—the process—has rescued my heart. Do
I miss those easy, fun times? Absolutely, like someone giving
up an addiction misses their vice of choice. But I am better

for taking this journey, for not giving up, and for not cling-
ing desperately to those things that didn't matter. . . . I pray
I can continue to focus on what truly matters and never rely
on those "treats" to get me through a day or take up so much
time in my life that it becomes my life. My life is here, being a
husband, father, leader, and son—and I will continue to focus
on my heavenly Father that has been giving us the power to
tell our mountains to move out of the way.[14]

Psalm 86:11 reads, "Teach me your way, LORD, that I may rely on
your faithfulness; give me an undivided heart, that I may fear your
name." When our own little indulgences no longer occupy large por-
tions of our hearts, we are that much closer to having the undivided
heart the psalmist refers to.

Now let's be clear. We're not saying it's wrong to take time to do
something you enjoy. In fact, it's vitally important that you take care
of yourself by doing whatever it is that refreshes you (see also "Strength
for the Fight," p. 156). Take an hour alone with a good book. Watch
a movie. Grab coffee or watch the ball game with friends. Date your
spouse! The indulgences we need to be wary of are those hobbies or habits that occupy so much of our affections that we rely on them instead
of God to carry us through.

Jeff Davidson noticed a dramatic change in his own heart as a result
of raising a son who has autism and cerebral palsy. Many people ask Jeff
if he feels robbed of all the experiences a father and typical son would
have. His response is that he has been robbed indeed, but not at all
the way most people would imagine. On his blog, he wrote a letter to
autism and cerebral palsy:

You've robbed me from my own pride, selfishness, and greed.
    You've robbed me from my tendency to put my work above
my family.

You've robbed me from living for myself instead of in service to others.

You've robbed me of only caring about those who are just like me.[15]

Jeff goes on explain that the disorders that could have destroyed his family, God has used to teach him unconditional love and grace, and how to find joy and be content in all things. "He has simply used them to draw me closer to Him, help me understand Him, and make me stronger through Him."

The psalmist wrote, "Search me, God, and know my heart; test me and know my anxious thoughts. See if there is any offensive way in me, and lead me in the way everlasting" (Ps. 139:23–24). When we surrender our "offensive ways" to God and allow him to set us free from them—when we shed harmful habits and faulty ways of thinking—we gain so much more than we are losing. An undivided heart brings us closer to the heart of Christ.

Dear Lord, search my heart and scrub it clean. If I am relying too much on anything other than you, prune those things away from me. May nothing claim more of my heart than you. In Jesus's name, amen.

DIGGING DEEPER

1. What do you rely on to get you through the day?
2. What faulty mind-set has God freed you from?
3. What have you given up during this season of life that has actually been like a jailbreak for your heart?

EIGHT

Branching Out
Touching Others' Lives
Through the Journey

My command is this: Love each other
as I have loved you.

JOHN 15:12

SPEAK UP

Jocelyn

Speak up for those who cannot speak for themselves,
for the rights of all who are destitute. Speak up and
judge fairly; defend the rights of the poor and needy.
PROVERBS 31:8-9

One spring Sunday, just getting to church was a victory for Tonya Nash. Not only was her husband deployed, but she had a newborn baby and a young autistic son, both of whom would have preferred staying home. But Tonya was running on empty and desperately in need of being filled up again in the way that only church can do.

When she took her son with autism to his classroom, however, Tonya learned that children's church was canceled for that day. "If I had known that I wouldn't have even come!" she blurted out, picturing the meltdown her son would certainly have if forced to enter the sanctuary with her. Exasperated, she stood there for a moment, wondering what to do.

"He can stay with us," the children's church coordinator told her, so Tonya left him with her at the check-in desk and went to the service.

A few weeks later, the children's church coordinator told Tonya she wanted to start a special-needs ministry at the church. By the time the

Nashes moved to their next military base, the ministry had been in place for a little more than a year, serving seven special children and their families on a weekly basis. The church became a forerunner in its county for special-needs ministry, often consulting with other churches that desired to start one as well.

Tonya could have bitten her tongue that day, neatly bottled up her frustrations, and marched back to her car. But she didn't, and a ministry was born.

Proverbs 31:8 tells us to "speak up for those who cannot speak for themselves." Tonya spoke for her own need, but she was also speaking on behalf of all the families who weren't there at the moment, the ones who found attending church difficult because there was no place for their children with special needs.

For the first two years after her son's diagnosis, Tonya didn't want to talk about it at all. Now, "speaking up" by sharing her testimony, resources, and support is second nature. "Part of God's plan for my life is to share what I've learned on this journey with other parents so they can make the world a better place for their children," she said.

Whether she's helping a church with their special-needs ministry, sharing resources for other parents through her blog, or conducting a social media campaign for Autism Awareness Month, Tonya has discovered that blessings flow both ways.

"When I'm helping others, it helps me too," she said. "It reminds me I'm not the only one dealing with these issues. The thought that I can help somebody else get through a situation I've been through is very fulfilling. Just like that lady at church stepped up and changed my life, it's a wonderful feeling to be able to do that for others."

Words are powerful. They can build up or tear down. As the parent of a child with unique needs, you have important things to say. Whether you are making others aware of the unique challenges your family faces, offering encouragement to other parents, or sharing your testimony as a believer, you have the power to edify and instruct in ways that others cannot. On the special-needs journey, there are so many things beyond your control. Speaking up at the right time and with the right words is well within it. "The mouths of the righteous utter wisdom, and their tongues speak what is just" (Ps. 37:30).

Lord, thank you for giving me a voice. Help me use it for your glory, as I "speak up for those who cannot speak for themselves." May my words fall on hearts that are ready to receive them. May my words encourage others and glorify you. In Jesus's name, amen.

DIGGING DEEPER

1. Do you find it easy or difficult to share your testimony? Why do you think that is?
2. If you could share one message with other parents of kids with special needs, what would it be?
3. If you could help other people understand one thing about the special-needs community, what would it be?

FRIENDS IN THE FIRE

Kimberly

The king's command was so urgent and the furnace
so hot that the flames of the fire killed the soldiers who
took up Shadrach, Meshach and Abednego, and these three
men, firmly tied, fell into the blazing furnace. Then King
Nebuchadnezzar leaped to his feet in amazement and asked his
advisers, "Weren't there three men that we tied up and threw
into the fire?" They replied, "Certainly, Your Majesty." He said,
"Look! I see four men walking around in the fire, unbound
and unharmed, and the fourth looks like a son of the gods."

DANIEL 3:22-25

I have some amazing friends. The kind you can call in the middle of
the night if you have to take someone to the hospital, or who don't
mind seeing your house when it looks like it could be declared a fed-
eral disaster area. They are the kinds of friends Shadrach, Meshach, and
Abednego were to each other in the Old Testament. When crisis came,
they held tight to Jesus and walked straight into the fire together.

My son once met another child whose sibling has special needs. I was
so excited that my son would have a friend who knew what it was like!
I was eager to meet the child's mom and begin what I'd hoped would

be a "friends in the fire" kind of relationship. However, this sweet mom can be very shy; I can tell she isn't comfortable letting people into her world. We can commiserate with each other about the hardships of parenting, but I still struggle to prove I can be a friend who would step into the fire with her. My heart wants to give her the love and hope of Christ and stand alongside of her in this battle, because she needs a Shadrach, Meshach, and Abednego.

Look around you. There may be a mom or dad in your own life who needs a friend like that—or like Jonathan. When David was fleeing from Saul, Jonathan continued to come to his aid time and time again. They swore friendship to each other and to each other's descendants. After Jonathan was killed, David took Jonathan's disabled son, Mephibosheth, into his own home and treated him as an heir (2 Sam. 9).

We can be a friend like Jonathan to someone. Or maybe we can be a friend like Paul was to the church in Rome. He wrote to them:

> God, whom I serve in my spirit in preaching the gospel of his Son, is my witness how constantly I remember you in my prayers at all times; and I pray that now at last by God's will the way may be opened for me to come to you.
>
> I long to see you so that I may impart to you some spiritual gift to make you strong—that is, that you and I may be mutually encouraged by each other's faith. (Rom. 1:9–12).

This is the kind of friendship we need to offer a world in need of the love, peace, and hope of Jesus Christ.

When our lives are swamped with the care of our children, we often look to others for relief. But may we never forget that there are others out there in need of the comfort we may be able to give (2 Cor. 1:3–4). They need friends like Shadrach, Meshach, and Abednego. Like Jonathan and Paul. They need a friend like you. May God help us to be the friend to others that he has been to us.

Father, help me to fully appreciate the friends you've given me to carry me through this journey of raising a child with special needs. Help me to have eyes that see others who need a friend, and to share with them the comfort you have so freely given me. In Jesus's name, amen.

DIGGING DEEPER

1. Who are your "in the fire" friends?
2. Is there someone in your life whom you could reach out to—someone who needs a friend?
3. What are some ways in which the love of Christ could transform their life?

DUSTY DOORWAYS

Kimberly

He has made everything beautiful in its time.
He has also set eternity in the human heart; yet no one
can fathom what God has done from beginning to end.
ECCLESIASTES 3:11

I wasn't trying to eavesdrop. But on an airplane one day, the person sitting next to me engaged a stranger across the aisle in a discussion about God. I listened curiously to his reasons for not believing in Christ. My ears perked up when he began to recount his sister's pregnancy concerns. She had been told there was a good chance her baby would be born with major brain damage. Though everything turned out fine, he wanted to know what kind of God would do that to an innocent baby. Well, let's just say I felt it was time to join in the conversation. Compassion willed him to listen carefully and to gently word his probing questions.

Each person's heart is full of rooms and doors. Every now and then, a locked door cracks open. A tiny ray of light peeks through the door frame, and scattered particles of dust stir and bounce around. Nothing is more thrilling to me than being there when a door in the heart of a nonbeliever suddenly opens, ever so slightly, to the truth of Christ. I believe that's what happened on the plane that day. The young man did not accept Christ on the airplane, but he opened the door of his heart enough to hear the truth of the good news because of my daughter.

The reality of our situation has plunged me into the depths of theology, sent me searching for God's truth to quiet and reconcile my many questions, and kept me lying awake countless nights. But this working out of my salvation has allowed me to softly and tenderly touch those difficult questions with complete strangers who unknowingly have eternity in their hearts.

I find great comfort in knowing that even though I don't have it all together, God can use my faith and understanding of him to share his Word and truth. Often questions revolving around our daughter spur conversations about God and what my husband and I believe. I am not one to shove my way through a cracked door. But I will stand when welcomed and lovingly share what I believe.

When I'm afraid of what might happen when I share my faith, I remember Luke 21:15: "I will give you words and wisdom that none of your adversaries will be able to resist or contradict." I draw on the promise that according to Ecclesiastes 3:11, God has set eternity in the hearts of men. Whether or not they realize it, God has instilled within them a desire to know what will happen to them when they die. Knowing that God put that question there, I am emboldened to speak openly and freely and without fear. I also cling to Isaiah 55:11, where God himself says, "So is my word that goes out from my mouth: It will not return to me empty, but will accomplish what I desire and achieve the purpose for which I sent it." It is never for nothing when we speak the truth from God's Word!

Maybe you have never considered your family's situation and trials as a way to reach others for Christ. Be looking and praying for opportunities to share your faith, because in Acts 1:8 we read, "You will receive power when the Holy Spirit comes on you; and you will be my witnesses in Jerusalem, and in all Judea and Samaria, and to the ends of the earth." Trust that God will give you the right words to share. Though there are many difficulties in raising our children with special needs, it is a blessing that their very existence provokes compassion. And compassion has a way of opening locked doors.

Lord, give me an open heart that is willing to share your truth. I praise you, and I ask you to use my special child to draw hearts to you. I know you'll give me the words to say, and that they will accomplish exactly what you intend them to. In Jesus's name, amen.

Digging Deeper

1. What questions do people raise about faith and God when they learn that you have a child with special needs?
2. Is there someone in your life who encourages you in your spiritual walk, who could coach you on how to share your faith more freely?
3. Describe a time when you shared (or see that you missed the opportunity to share) your faith with a friend, family member, or even a stranger. What was the result?

WAVES OF KINDNESS

Jocelyn

Let us consider how we may spur one another on
toward love and good deeds.
HEBREWS 10:24

When Waverly McNeil turned ten years old, she received more than one thousand birthday cards, and rightly so. She and her little brother, Oliver, were both diagnosed with Sanfilippo syndrome, a genetic condition with a typical life span between twelve and eighteen years of age. Birthdays in the McNeil house are bittersweet.

For Waverly's eleventh birthday, her parents, Matt and Shannon, decided to make an unusual request through a special Facebook page called *Wavey Inspires*: No cards. Just kindness.

To honor their little girl's life, the McNeils asked everyone who "liked" the Facebook page to reach out to a family in their community who has a child with special needs. "Having a child with special needs can feel very isolating for some families," they explained on the page. "A smile and a friendly gesture can mean the world to them. We would love to see 'Waves of Kindness and Inclusion' across the world to honor sweet Waverly."[1]

The McNeils could have turned inward for Waverly's eleventh

birthday as they stepped one year closer to their daughter's passing. Instead they created an opportunity to spur others toward love and good deeds (Heb. 10:24).

It worked.

One woman bought gift cards for a family with a special-needs son so the parents could have a few date nights. At a department store, another woman noticed a mom pushing a little girl with special needs in the shopping cart, and she immediately bought that mom a Starbucks Frappuccino. Another family paid the bill at a restaurant so a special family dined for free. Some were inspired to donate to special-needs classrooms in their community, or to a fund for research for the cure.

In honor of Waverly, a woman spent an hour with an acquaintance whose son has no immune system, navigating through medical bills and providing counsel on which charges were illegal. That one meeting showed the family how they could potentially save $50,000. Another woman decided to step outside her comfort zone, with a plate of chocolate chip cookies in hand, and introduce herself to a neighboring family whose son has Down syndrome.

The list goes on. We'll never know the ripple effect of these Waves of Kindness and Inclusion. But we do know the McNeils touched lives when they chose to celebrate Wavey by encouraging others to honor the special-needs families in their own communities.

In essence, the McNeils were saying, "If you love our daughter, show love to others." In the same way, if we love God's Son, we also must show love to others. "A new command I give you: Love one another. As I have loved you, so you must love one another. By this everyone will know that you are my disciples, if you love one another" (John 13:34–35). The Lord has also made it clear that we are to show kindness to those who may be considered unworthy or unlovable—and in so doing, we are showing kindness to Christ. "Truly I tell you, whatever you did for one of the least of these brothers and sisters of mine, you did for me" (Matt. 25:40).

Loving others is a hallmark of our faith. When we, like the McNeils, can find ways to encourage kindness in others as well, the Lord is pleased indeed.

Lord, open my eyes to the ways my family can inspire kindness and inclusion in others. Help me love my own neighbor, whether it's a family that is walking a similar road as mine or one that has no clue what it's like for us and doesn't seem to care. Give me your perspective, your words, and your timing. In Jesus's name, amen.

DIGGING DEEPER
1. How might your family be able to encourage kindness in others?
2. Name one family you could consider reaching out to.
3. What is one thing you can do this week to show kindness to someone outside your family?

WORDS THAT MATTER

Kimberly

In your hearts revere Christ as Lord. Always be prepared
to give an answer to everyone who asks you to give the
reason for the hope that you have. But do this with
gentleness and respect.

1 PETER 3:15

The tension in the room came to a sudden climax. It felt like every eye in the room was on me. But in reality, only one person was looking at me, and the only one who felt any tension at all was me. The party was happening all around me, kids were running everywhere, and adults were mingling. I found myself in a conversation with someone I didn't know very well but who was well acquainted with my family and our daughter. We were discussing the local high school graduation when she said, "I don't understand why those kids from the special-needs program get a diploma. They didn't do the work and they aren't actually graduating. It's so uncomfortable to watch them go across the stage."

I felt all the blood drain out of my face and into my clenched fists. The worst part was that I had nothing to say. I was so shocked at the ignorance and insensitivity of the comment that I could hardly breathe.

On another occasion, this time on a family vacation, a man sitting on a bench right next to us started making fun of one of his friends. The crowd with him started laughing along when he began to mimic the walk of a disabled person. Here I was, merely three feet away, with my disabled child and my other children watching. I promptly stood up to confront him. I did my best to do it in love and to be gracious, but the mom inside me was hurting for my child and her siblings.

Whether circumstances involve an acquaintance, a stranger, or even a friend or family member, we are all going to find ourselves in similar situations where we wonder why someone would say or do something so hurtful. Our children are dear to us, and when someone insults them, we have every right to be offended. It's what we do with that offense that speaks to the world about our faith.

In Ecclesiastes 7:21–22 we are advised, "Do not pay attention to every word people say, or you may hear your servant cursing you—for you know in your heart that many times you yourself have cursed others." First Corinthians 13:4–7 tells us, "Love is patient, love is kind. It does not envy, it does not boast, it is not proud. It does not dishonor others, it is not self-seeking, it is not easily angered, it keeps no record of wrongs. Love does not delight in evil but rejoices with the truth. It always protects, always trusts, always hopes, always perseveres."

I was challenged by a sermon recently that asked me to take out the word "love" and put in my own name. Kimberly is patient. Kimberly is kind. Can we say these things about ourselves? When dealing with an offense, can I say with honesty that Kimberly is not easily angered and keeps no record of wrongs? It is a good litmus test for how to deal with people and situations like the ones I've described.

When we handle these sensitive and difficult moments as parents, we always have an opportunity to point back to the cross. The man making fun of the walk of a disabled person was truly mortified and disgusted with his behavior and asked for my forgiveness. This opened the door for me to tell him about how much Christ has forgiven me.

Remember that before Christ, we were the mockers and the scorners. We were the offenders, yet Christ in his great mercy reached out to us. With arms wide open on the cross, he gave his life to show his great love for humanity. With reverence for Christ, gentleness, and respect, we can be prepared in any situation, even if the situation has been hurtful to us, to give the reason for the hope that we have.

Father, forgive me for being so easily angered and for forgetting that my sin is offensive to you. Help me to respond with respect and gentleness when someone is hurtful or ignorant regarding my child. Help me point back to your character and the hope I have in you. In Jesus's name, amen.

DIGGING DEEPER

1. When have you been offended by an insensitive comment directed at the special-needs community?
2. How did you respond?
3. How could you respond in the future?

THE GIFT OF PRESENCE

Jocelyn

[Job's friends] sat on the ground with him for seven
days and seven nights. No one said a word to him,
because they saw how great his suffering was.

JOB 2:13

Job's friends had one shining moment. It lasted an entire week.
For seven days and seven nights, they sat silently on the ground
with Job. No words were adequate. Nor were they necessary. The friends
didn't ask for cushions or places at the table. Instead, they were on the
ground with Job, sitting among the ashes with torn robes and dust on
their heads. For *seven days*.

Presence is a gift. Job's friends couldn't possibly understand how he
was feeling. But you can very likely understand exactly how another
special-needs parent is feeling if you are a little further down the road
on your own journey. We are marked by our trials. Being wounded
opens our eyes to the suffering of others.

When Laurie Wallin sees another mom in a doctor's or therapist's
waiting room with tears in her eyes and a faraway look on her face,
Laurie doesn't tell that tearful mom to buy Laurie's book, *Get Your Joy
Back*. She offers her a tissue and puts her arm around her shoulders.

"There's a quietness that's grown in my heart," Laurie said. "A general sense of empathy no matter what kind of pain. Now I'm OK by encouraging others by my presence instead of filling the silence with words. People have responded to that by saying that was the most important encouragement they received."

Sometimes, however, this ministry costs us. This was certainly the case for Alice Wisler when she learned her friend Cres was hospitalized and that her body was shutting down with sepsis. Fifteen years earlier, Alice's four-year-old son Daniel had gone into sepsis right before his death. "I don't do hospitals," Alice reasoned as she decided not to visit. It was just too hard. Too much.

But one day, Alice was unable to resist the pull to go. Not just for her friend Cres, but for Cres's mother, who had arrived from Swaziland to watch her daughter die. So she went after all.

A silent Cres lay with the buzzing machines surrounding her, and to her right sat her mother on a chair, a little woman with a balled up tissue. A little woman with pain the size of Montana. How I knew that agony! . . . Before leaving, I had to hug this woman. As she stood up to meet me, we embraced. Her arms grew tight around me; I didn't want to let her go.

When I got to the hospital parking deck, I toppled into my Jeep and let those tears out. I cried for Cres's family, for the unfairness of illness, and yes, I sobbed because, even after all these years, I still miss my son. . . . I hope [Cres's mom] felt the connection of mother-to-mother grieving. But most of all, I felt I had gone to the hospital out of obedience to God, allowing Him to care for me as I showed compassion for others.[2]

The Bible tells us to "be sympathetic, love one another, be compassionate and humble" (1 Peter 3:8). May we remember that by our presence, we can demonstrate all of these things.

As we contemplate the gift of presence, Jesus is our ultimate example. He is Immanuel, God with us. "The Word became flesh and made his dwelling among us" (John 1:14). He will never leave us. "Surely I am with you always, to the very end of the age" (Matt. 28:20). May we find comfort and peace in his presence even as we compassionately spend time with others.

Immanuel, thank you for dwelling among us and sending your Comforter, the Holy Spirit. Remind me of your presence daily, even hourly. Show me where my presence would be a blessing to another, and give me the courage to offer that gift. In Jesus's name, amen.

Digging Deeper

1. When were you very encouraged by someone? How did he or she encourage you?
2. Who in your life may need a similar encouragement now?
3. In the next week or so, with whom do you plan to be present?

BUDDY SYSTEM

Kimberly

Two are better than one, because they have a good return
for their labor: If either of them falls down, one can help the
other up. But pity anyone who falls and has no one
to help them up.

ECCLESIASTES 4:9-10

Our church has a buddy system that pairs children with special
needs with an adult or college student to be their helper so parents
can attend Sunday school. We have heard many stories of buddies feeling incredibly blessed to be with our children. They look forward to it
and grow to love the children, welcoming them into their lives and our
church. The buddy system is one way churches can be obedient to Jesus.
"Jesus called the children to him and said, 'Let the little children come
to me, and do not hinder them, for the kingdom of God belongs to such
as these. Truly I tell you, anyone who will not receive the kingdom of
God like a little child will never enter it'" (Luke 18:16–17).

Not only does Jesus have a heart for children, but he has a heart for
the disabled. In Luke 14:12–14, he advises a Pharisee, "'When you give
a luncheon or dinner, do not invite your friends, your brothers or sisters, your relatives, or your rich neighbors; if you do, they may invite

you back and so you will be repaid. But when you give a banquet, invite the poor, the crippled, the lame, the blind, and you will be blessed. Although they cannot repay you, you will be repaid at the resurrection of the righteous." Then he tells the parable of the great banquet, in which the host, desiring his house to be full, sends his servant into the streets to bring in the poor, the crippled, the blind, and the lame (vv. 15–23).

God's desire is for the outcasts to be drawn in, for those on the margins to come to the table and participate in community. The buddy system that many churches use is one excellent way to do that. But the buddy system isn't just for worship services, and it isn't just for our children. When we come alongside another struggling parent, God is very pleased indeed.

Ecclesiastes 4:9–10 tells us, "Two are better than one, because they have a good return for their labor: If either of them falls down, one can help the other up. But pity anyone who falls and has no one to help them up." When we engage in a buddy system with other parents, we extend helping hands to lift them up.

After years of struggling to accept that his son has autism, Chad Shelley actively advocates for families who are also touched by the autism spectrum. While he serves as president of the regional chapter of the autism support group, his wife, Allison, offers support on a more personal level. "My role is more one-on-one, reaching out to new moms, new families," she said. "It has allowed me to share my faith in ways I never would have been presented with or felt comfortable doing. Because our son has autism, we've been put in a position to help other people. It has become our purpose, our way of giving back. How can we help others who are struggling?"

Even those of us who aren't comfortable with public speaking can pair up with another parent and offer prayer and encouragement. One of the greatest gifts you can give to another person is the assurance that he or she is not alone.

Dear Lord, your love for those who are considered weak in this world is beyond what I could ever imagine. I praise you that these children have a seat at your banquet table! Open my eyes to see which family or parent might need some personal encouragement. Give me the words to say, and the grace to listen well as they share. Use me as a vessel of your love for them. In Jesus's name, amen.

DIGGING DEEPER

1. What steps could you take to start a buddy system for children with special needs at your church?

2. Who has acted as a buddy for you by offering encouragement and guidance when you needed it most? Consider sending that person a thank-you note so they know how much their care meant to you.

3. Who in your life might need you to come alongside them in this season? What is one simple way you could do that this week?

JILL'S HOUSE

Jocelyn

Though you have made me see troubles, many and bitter,
you will restore my life again; from the depths
of the earth you will again bring me up.
PSALM 71:20

As Brenda Solomon sat on the floor with her daughter, waiting for Jill's next seizure, Brenda wondered if her own tears would ever cease to fall. The relentless seizures were burning out Jill's brain. The future seemed like one dark, endless tunnel of exhaustion and grief.

"God!" she wept. "I am at the absolute end of myself! I don't know what to do. The only thing I ask is that You use Jill in a mighty way, because this hurts so much, and I don't want to waste this pain!"[3]

It seems odd to Brenda now that she had asked God to use Jill, a small disabled girl, instead of herself, a pastor's wife. But God would use Jill in a mighty way indeed.

A few hours after Brenda's desperate plea, she received a phone call. By the end of the conversation, the woman on the other end had made a plan to organize some caregivers for Jill.

"Respite gave us hope," Brenda shared. "It changed our lives. I don't know where we'd be today if we hadn't gotten it. Lon says he doubts he'd still be in the ministry; perhaps our marriage wouldn't have survived. I doubt we could have weathered the storm of Jill's disabilities without the grace of God, expressed through His people helping us."[4]

In 2010, the Solomons founded Jill's House to offer overnight respite care to hundreds of disabled children a month. The 42,000-square-foot "respite resort" provides care for intellectually disabled children ages six through seventeen. While parents get a chance to reconnect as a couple, devote time to their other children, work on degree programs, visit with friends, or tackle home projects, the children at Jill's House are having a blast with staff and volunteers who not only care for their needs but truly love them.

Just as respite care gave the Solomons hope, now Jill's House is breathing life into other families. Tricia and Dick Schmehl "were dying inside. We lived in a cocoon, exhausted, with no one to turn to." They were about to give up.

Then they learned about Jill's House, which has proven to be as exciting for their disabled teenager as a trip to Disney World. "Since Jill's House came into our lives, we have been able to reconnect all of our relationships—to ourselves as individuals, as a couple, and as parents to Tori. Jill's House saved our lives."[5]

Jill's House offers both respite and hospitality. Even if you are unable to offer respite care to another family, can you offer hospitality? Tricia's description of living in a cocoon is all too fitting for the isolated special-needs family. Yet we were created to live in community with others. "Share with the Lord's people who are in need. Practice hospitality" (Rom. 12:13). First Peter 4:9 puts a finer point on it for the reluctant among us: "Offer hospitality to one another without grumbling."

One of the biggest benefits of Jill's House, as Tricia testified, is that it allows parents to restore their marital relationships and their relationships with their typical children, and it nurtures friendships between children attending Jill's House at the same time. When we practice hospitality, aren't we also nurturing relationships? Our homes need not be picture-perfect. The food needn't be fancy—or even part of the fellow-ship at all. Open arms, open hearts, and open conversations are restor-ative on their own merits.

Brenda Solomon's prayer for God to use her daughter was answered with Jill's House. What can God do with your house?

Lord, I know the loneliness this lifestyle brings. Use me and my home to help banish isolation for another family. Open my eyes and ears to opportunities to embrace others no matter where they are on the journey. Restore our lives again. In Jesus's name, amen.

DIGGING DEEPER

1. When was the last time you had people other than your family in your home?
2. What is one thing that has prevented you from inviting people over?
3. The next time you have guests, what will your primary goal be for how they feel?

SHARE YOUR STORY

Kimberly

Then Jesus came to them and said, "All authority in heaven
and on earth has been given to me. Therefore go and make
disciples of all nations, baptizing them in the name of the
Father and of the Son and of the Holy Spirit, and teaching
them to obey everything I have commanded you. And
surely I am with you always, to the very end of the age."

MATTHEW 28:18-20

Each year the students in our youth ministry apply to go on mission
trips. As a part of the application they are asked to give a brief testimony about how they came to have a relationship with Christ, and
what he is doing in their life now. Each year, lives impacted by the gospel of Jesus spread out across the globe to share what our friend Pastor
David Johnson says is "the greatest story ever told, about the greatest
person who ever lived, about the greatest need ever met, and the greatest price ever paid."

As parents of children with special needs, we may not have the freedom to travel the globe or even leave our county to share the gospel.
But the desperate need for Christ is everywhere, and our call from Jesus
in Matthew 28 is clear. When we find ourselves with other parents

like us at doctor's offices or in hospital waiting rooms, we can look for open doors to share the hope we have in Christ. Sometimes even our own extended families are in desperate need of it. First Peter 3:15 tells us, "Always be prepared to give an answer to everyone who asks you to give the reason for the hope that you have. But do this with gentleness and respect."

Having an answer means someone has asked the question. Many times, answering questions about Abbey has opened the door to more spiritual conversations. An openness about raising your child with special needs has the potential to touch lives. Jesus said in Matthew 5:14– 16, "You are the light of the world. A town built on a hill cannot be hidden. Neither do people light a lamp and put it under a bowl. Instead they put it on its stand, and it gives light to everyone in the house. In the same way, let your light shine before others, that they may see your good deeds and glorify your Father in heaven." If you're afraid that your light is too small, listen to what missionary Bob McKemey says: "My Christian walk may not be a spotlight, maybe just a candle; but even candles are meant to bring light to dark places."

What is this candle all about? It's about living a life that is Christ centered. Philippians 2:3–8 gives a picture of what this looks like:

> Do nothing out of selfish ambition or vain conceit. Rather, in humility value others above yourselves, not looking to your own interests but each of you to the interests of the others.
>
> In your relationships with one another, have the same mind-set as Christ Jesus:
>
> Who, being in very nature God, did not consider equality with God something to be used to his own advantage; rather, he made himself nothing by taking the very nature of a servant, being made in human likeness. And being found in appearance as a man, he humbled himself by becoming obedient to death—even death on a cross!

As we go about first loving God and then loving others as Christ loved us, our story draws people in, giving us a chance to be a candle in the darkness. Evangelism is a process, and the results belong to God.[6]

Dear Lord, I pray for opportunities to share my faith in you. Open doors to talk about you with those around me who don't know you. I pray that you would give me an open heart to share my story. I trust you with the rest. In Jesus's name, amen.

DIGGING DEEPER

1. How has your life been changed by receiving Jesus Christ as your Savior?
2. Whom can you pray for that needs to hear about the love of Jesus?
3. In what ways can you be more open or grow in your ability to share your story?

KNOWING JESUS PERSONALLY

If you have not yet trusted Christ as your Savior, let today be the day that you invite him to be Lord of your life. Without Christ, we have no hope in this life and no hope of enjoying heaven in the next. But because of Christ, we can accept eternal life as a free gift based on God's grace.

> For the wages of sin is death, but the gift of God is eternal life in Christ Jesus our Lord. (Rom. 6:23)

Heaven is not something that we can earn or deserve on our own merits. We can't go to church enough, give enough money to charity, or be good enough in any way to pave our own way to heaven. But the good news is that we don't have to—because God's grace is offered to us as a gift.

> For it is by grace you have been saved, through faith—and this is not from yourselves, it is the gift of God—not by works, so that no one can boast. (Eph. 2:8–9)

No one deserves to go to heaven, because we sin. Even the best of us do things that displease God.

All have turned away, they have together become worthless; there
is no one who does good, not even one. . . . For all have sinned
and fall short of the glory of God. (Rom. 3:12, 23)

For whoever keeps the whole law and yet stumbles at just one
point is guilty of breaking all of it. (James 2:10)

Because God is holy and just, our sin prevents us from being able to
be in his presence.

For the wages of sin is death. (Rom. 6:23)

Because God also is not willing that any should perish, he sent his
Son, Jesus Christ, into the world as the perfect, blameless one to die for
us. He paid the penalty for our sins and purchased a place in heaven
for us.

But God demonstrates his own love for us in this: While we
were still sinners, Christ died for us. (Rom. 5:8)

For Christ also suffered once for sins, the righteous for the
unrighteous, to bring you to God. He was put to death in the
body but made alive in the Spirit. (1 Peter 3:18)

Jesus answered, "I am the way and the truth and the life. No
one comes to the Father except through me." (John 14:6)

If you believe this much is true, you're on the right track. But you
must go one step further and receive the gift of salvation by placing
your personal faith in Christ, asking him to be your Savior and Lord.
Faith is turning from your sins and trusting in Jesus Christ alone for
your eternal salvation.

Yet to all who did receive him, to those who believed in his name,
he gave the right to become children of God. (John 1:12)

"Everyone who calls on the name of the Lord will be saved."
(Rom. 10:13)

Are you ready to invite Christ into your life? Pray to him right now,
acknowledging your sin and accepting the free gift of eternal life. Ask
him to show you how to live in a way that honors him. The suggested
prayer below may express the desire of your heart:

> *Dear Lord, thank you for the gift of eternal life. I know I am a*
> *sinner and that I cannot save myself. I believe Jesus is the Son of*
> *God and that he died for my sins and rose again from the dead.*
> *I now put my complete trust in him alone for eternal life. Thank*
> *you for saving me. Now, help me through your Holy Spirit to live*
> *a life that honors you. In Jesus's name, amen.*

If you prayed to receive Christ, celebrate! You just made the most
important decision that you will ever make in your life. Find someone
to share your news with, and seek out a Bible-teaching church where
you can spend time with other Christians and learn the Word of God.
Make Bible reading and prayer a daily priority, and allow God to mold
you into the person he wants you to be.

NOTES

Any undocumented stories and quotes from individuals in this book are from private interviews conducted by the authors. In each case, the persons and events portrayed have been used with permission. To protect the privacy of these individuals, some of the names and identifying details have been changed.

Part One. Uprooted: When Life's Landscape Changes

1. Ellen Stumbo, "We Belong Together," *Hope and Encouragement for the Special Needs Parent* (blog), October 12, 2012, http://www.ellenstumbo .com/we-belong-together/.

2. Adapted from Ellen Stumbo, "A Parent's Unconditional Love, or More Than I Can Handle?," *Hope and Encouragement for the Special Needs Parent* (blog), October 24, 2012, http://www.ellenstumbo.com/a-parents -unconditional-love-or-more-than-i-can-handle/.

3. Ibid.

4. Ellen Stumbo, "I Choose Love," *Hope and Encouragement for the Special Needs Parent* (blog), October 25, 2012, http://www.ellenstumbo.com/i -choose-love/.

5. Ibid.

6. Ibid.

7. Gillian Marchenko, *Sun Shine Down: A Memoir* (Ossining, NY: T. S. Poetry Press, 2013), 121.

8. Jared Buckley, "Struggle Does Not Mean Discouraged," *Building Special*

Families (blog), http://specialfamiliescoach.com/struggle-does-not-mean
-discouraged.

9. Laura Slezak, "The Wake of Mother's Day," *A Way in the Wild* (blog), May
11, 2015, http://wayinthewild.blogspot.com/2015/05/the-wake-of-moth
ers-day.html.

10. Marchenko, *Sun Shine Down*, 83–84.

11. Jeff Davidson, *No More Peanut Butter Sandwiches: A Father, a Son with
Special Needs, and Their Journey with God* (Castle Rock, OH: Crosslink,
2014), 39.

12. Shannon McNeil, "Identity," *For Waverly, For Oliver, For a Cure* (blog),
July 31, 2015, http://familymctravels.blogspot.com/2015/07/identity.html.

13. Jennifer Rothschild, *Walking by Faith: Lessons Learned in the Dark*
(Nashville: Lifeway, 2003), 17.

Part Two. Sowing Seeds: Cultivating Truth and Faith

1. All quotes in this devotion, except for those from Scripture, are from
Ellen Stumbo, "Trusting God in the Midst of Trials," *Hope and Encouragement for the Special Needs Parent* (blog), February 3, 2015, http://
www.ellenstumbo.com/trusting-god-in-the-midst-of-trials/.

2. Lon Solomon, *Brokenness: How God Redeems Pain and Suffering* (San Francisco: Purple Pomegranate Productions, 2010), Kindle edition, loc. 285.

3. Jeff Davidson, "Seven Minutes," *Goodnight Superman* (blog), May 22,
2015, http://goodnightsuperman.com/seven-minutes/.

4. Jeff Davidson, *No More Peanut Butter Sandwiches: A Father, a Son with
Special Needs, and Their Journey with God* (Castle Rock, OH: Crosslink,
2014), 6.

5. Ibid., 33.

Part Three. Pulling Weeds: Digging Out That Which Entangles

1. Laura Slezak, "Not Failing, Just Succeeding Half Way," *A Way in the Wild*
(blog), June 2, 2015, http://wayinthewild.blogspot.com/2015/06/not
-failing-just-succeeding-half-way.html.

2. Gillian Marchenko, *Sun Shine Down: A Memoir* (Ossining, NY: T. S. Poetry Press, 2013), 124.

3. Brian Riley as quoted in "From Grief to Guilt to Sheer Joy," Jill's House website, *Family Spotlight* newsletter, May 2015, http://archive.constant contact.com/fs189/1101794284957/archive/1121181886279.html.

4. Anne-Marie Wurzel, "Church!" *Rob & Anne-Marie* (blog), July 29, 2015, http://www.robandannemarie.com/2015/07/church/.

5. Gillian Marchenko, "Letting Go of Self-Sabotage," *Gillian Marchenko* (blog), March 18, 2015, http://www.gillianmarchenko.com/letting-go-of -self-sabotage/.

6. Anne-Marie Wurzel, "Comparison Is a Thief," *Rob & Anne-Marie* (blog), May 28, 2015, http://www.robandannemarie.com/2015/05/comparison -is-a-thief/.

7. Barb Dittrich, "The Sibling Saga I Didn't Anticipate," *Comfort in the Midst of Chaos* (blog), September 4, 2015, http://www.comfortinthemidst ofchaos.com/2015/09/the-sibling-saga-i-didnt-anticipate.html.

8. Ibid.

9. Anne-Marie Wurzel, "GA-1 Mind Games," *Rob & Ann-Marie* (blog), January 27, 2015, http://www.robandannemarie.com/2015/01/ga-1-mind -games/.

Part Four. Parched: When Hope Withers

1. All quotations in this devotional adapted from Rebekah Benimoff, "The Calling," *Just Me Mama* (blog), October 27, 2012, http://justmemama .blogspot.com/2012/10/the-calling.html.

2. Laurie Wallin, "When the Pain Means We're Healing," *Laurie Wallin* (blog), March 25, 2015, http://lauriewallin.com/wordpress/when-the -pain-means-were-healing/.

3. Kathryn Sneed, "Medical-Related PTSD Part Two: Special Needs Caregiver Trauma," *Singing Through the Rain* (blog), June 2, 2015, http:// www.singingthroughtherain.net/2015/06/medical-related-ptsd-part -two-special-needs-caregiver-trauma.html.

4. Barb Dittrich, "8 Truths About PTSD in Parents of Kids with Special Needs," *Different Dream Living* (blog), April 24, 2015, http://different dream.com/2015/04/8-truths-about-ptsd-in-parents-of-kids-with -special-needs/.

5. Children can suffer from medically related traumatic stress too. For more information on this topic, see Jolene Philo, *Does My Child Have PTSD? What to Do When Your Child Is Hurting from the Inside Out* (Sanger, CA: Familius, 2015); or search her website and blog, *Different Dream Living*, http://differentdream.com.

6. Jolene Philo, *A Different Dream for My Child: Meditations for Parents of Critically or Chronically Ill Children* (Grand Rapids: Discovery House, 2009), 195.

7. Ibid., 197.

8. Alane Pearce, "Out of the Darkness," in Jocelyn Green, *Faith Deployed . . . Again: More Daily Encouragement for Military Wives* (Chicago: Moody Publishers, 2011), 136.

9. Alane Pearce, *Notes from the Margins: Healing Conversations with God* (Colorado Springs: Corbin Press, 2009), 141.

10. Pearce, "Out of the Darkness," in Green, *Faith Deployed . . . Again*, 137.

11. Kathryn Sneed, "Struggling," *Singing Through the Rain* (blog), posted May 30, 2013, http://www.singingthroughtherain.net/2013/05/struggl ing.html.

12. Laurie Wallin, *Get Your Joy Back: Banishing Resentment and Reclaiming Confidence in Your Special Needs Family* (Grand Rapids: Kregel, 2015), 145.

13. Ibid., 150–51.

14. Ibid., 152.

Part Five. Drenched: Nourishing the Soul

1. Jeff Davidson, *No More Peanut Butter Sandwiches: A Father, a Son with Special Needs, and Their Journey with God* (Castle Rock, OH: Crosslink, 2014), 116.

2. Ibid., 119.

3. Laura Slezak, "Best Daddy Ever," *A Way in the Wild* (blog), January 25, 2015, http://wayinthewild.blogspot.com/2015/01/best-daddy-ever.html.

4. Davidson, *No More Peanut Butter Sandwiches*, 111.

5. Wendy Hilton, "Caring for Yourself While Caring for Your Special Needs Child," *The Busy Mom* (blog), November 20, 2014, http://heidistjohn .com/parenting/caring-for-yourself-while-caring-for-your-special-needs -child.

6. John Piper, "Do Not Grow Weary in Well-Doing," Desiring God website, http://www.desiringgod.org/sermons/do-not-grow-weary-in-well-doing.

7. Laurie Wallin, *Get Your Joy Back: Banishing Resentment and Reclaiming Confidence in Your Special Needs Family* (Grand Rapids: Kregel, 2015), 76.

8. Gillian Marchenko, "Hard Earned Love," *Pulling to Stand: Glimpses of Parenting Two Children with Down Syndrome Down Very Different Paths* (Gillian Marchenko, 2014), 16, http://www.gillianmarchenko.com /wp-content/uploads/2014/09/Pulling-to-Stand2.pdf.

9. *Merriam-Webster's Collegiate Dictionary*, 16th ed., s.v. "indispensable."

10. Greg Lucas, "Indispensable," *Not Alone* (blog), August 13, 2013, http:// specialneedsparenting.net/indispensable-autism/.

11. Wendy Hilton, "Loving and Living with Your Special Needs Child," *The Busy Mom* (blog), December 4, 2014, http://heidistjohn.com/parenting /loving-and-living-with-your-special-needs-child.

Part Six. Sunlit: Turning Toward the Son

1. Kathryn Sneed, "When God Seems Silent," *Singing Through the Rain* (blog), April 5, 2015, http://www.singingthroughtherain.net/2015/04 /when-god-seems-silent.html.

2. See *Merriam-Webster's*, s.v. "declare."

3. Gillian Marchenko, "Hard Earned Love," *Pulling to Stand: Glimpses of Parenting Two Children with Down Syndrome Down Very Different Paths* (Gillian Marchenko, 2014), 16, http://www.gillianmarchenko.com /wp-content/uploads/2014/09/Pulling-to-Stand2.pdf.

4. Ann Spangler, *Praying the Names of Jesus: A Daily Guide* (Grand Rapids: Zondervan, 2006), 252.

5. Sue and Hector Badeau, *Are We There Yet?: The Ultimate Road Trip: Adopting and Raising 22 Kids* (Franklin, TN: Carpenter's Son, 2013), Kindle edition, loc. 4286.

Part Seven. Pruned: When Pain Produces Fruit

1. Greg Lucas, *Wrestling with an Angel: A Story of Love, Disability, and the Lessons of Grace* (Hudson, OH: Cruciform Press, 2010), Kindle edition, loc. 227.

2. Ibid., Kindle edition, loc. 246.

3. Ibid., Kindle edition, loc. 250.

4. Ibid., Kindle edition, loc. 199.

5. Leslie Vernick, *How to Act Right When Your Spouse Acts Wrong* (Colorado Springs: Waterbrook, 2013).

6. Barb Dittrich, "Rediscovering Who I Am," *Comfort in the Midst of Chaos* (blog), September 8, 2015, http://www.comfortinthemidstofchaos .com/2015/09/rediscovering-who-i-am.html.

7. Lucas, *Wrestling with an Angel*, Kindle edition, loc. 338.

8. Ibid., Kindle edition, loc. 405.

9. Ibid., Kindle edition, loc. 325.

10. Lon Solomon, *Brokenness: How God Redeems Pain and Suffering* (San Francisco: Purple Pomegranate Productions, 2010), Kindle edition, loc. 647.

11. Anne-Marie Wurzel, "Why Reagan?," *Rob & Anne-Marie* (blog), March 29, 2015, http://www.robandannemarie.com/2015/03/why-reagan/.

12. Solomon, *Brokenness*, Kindle edition, loc. 1319.

13. Nancy Leigh DeMoss, *Surrender: The Heart God Controls* (Chicago: Moody, 2003), 59.

14. Rob Wurzel, "Jailbreak for My Heart," *Rob & Anne-Marie* (blog), February 26, 2015, http://www.robandannemarie.com/2015/02/jailbreak-for-my -heart/.

15. Jeff Davidson, "I've Been Robbed . . . So Thanks," *Goodnight Superman*

(blog), March 27, 2015, http://goodnightsuperman.com/ive-been-robbed
-so-thanks/.

Part Eight. Branching Out: Touching Others' Lives Through the Journey

1. *Wavey Inspires* (Facebook page), accessed July 7, 2015, http://www.face
   book.com/waveyinspires.
2. Alice J. Wisler, *Getting Out of Bed in the Morning: Reflections of Comfort in Heartache* (Abilene, TX: Leafwood, 2013), Kindle edition, loc. 889.
3. Brenda Solomon, "HOPE! A Message from Jill's Mom, Brenda Solomon, Cofounder of Jill's House," Jill's House website, http://jillshouse.org/a
   -message-from-jills-mom/.
4. Ibid.
5. Tricia Schmehl, "Jill's House Saved Our Lives," Jill's House website, *Family Spotlight* newsletter, October 2013, http://archive.constantcon
   tact.com/fs189/1101794284957/archive/1115456191156. html#schmehl.
6. If you need help with sharing your faith or answering the questions commonly asked about Christianity, www.searchministries.org has tools to help you.

RESOURCES

While there are many resources available that are specific to a particular special need, we'd like to share with you some that are relevant no matter what your child's diagnosis is. This is not an exhaustive list, just some of our personal favorites. We encourage you to find other need-specific resources, whether those are books, websites, blogs, Facebook groups, or national foundations.

BOOKS
For you as a parent
Fuller, Cheri and Louise Tucker Jones. *Extraordinary Kids: Nurturing and Championing Your Child with Special Needs.* Colorado Springs: Focus on the Family Publishers, 1997.

Philo, Jolene. *The Caregivers Notebook: An Organizational Tool and Support to Help You Care for Others.* Grand Rapids: Discovery House, 2014.

———. *A Different Dream for My Child: Meditations for Parents of Critically or Chronically Ill Children.* Grand Rapids: Discovery House, 2009.

———. *Different Dream Parenting: A Practical Guide to Raising a Child with Special Needs.* Grand Rapids: Discovery House, 2011.

———. *Does My Child Have PTSD?: What to Do When Your Child Is Hurting from the Inside Out*. Sanger, CA: Familius, 2015.

Wallin, Laurie. *Get Your Joy Back: Banishing Resentment and Reclaiming Confidence in Your Special Needs Family*. Grand Rapids: Kregel, 2015.

Wisler, Alice J. *Getting Out of Bed in the Morning: Reflections of Comfort in Heartache*. Abilene, TX: Leafwood, 2013.

For you and your church

Hubach, Stephanie O. *Same Lake, Different Boat: Coming Alongside People Touched by Disability*. Phillipsburg, NJ: P & R Publishing, 2006.

Special Needs, Special Ministry. Foreword by Joni Eareckson Tada. Loveland, CO: Group Publishing, 2003.

Wetherbee, Katie and Jolene Philo. *Every Child Welcome: A Ministry Handbook for Including Kids with Special Needs*. Grand Rapids: Kregel, 2015.

For you as a spouse

Chapman, Gary. *The Five Love Languages: The Secret to Love That Lasts*. Revised edition. Chicago: Northfield, 2015.

Vernick, Leslie. *How to Act Right When Your Spouse Acts Wrong*. Colorado Springs: Waterbrook, 2013.

WEBSITES

Different Dream Living: For Those Caring for a Loved One with Special Needs

DifferentDream.com. This is the website of author Jolene Philo, who offers resources and blog posts for parents of chronically and critically ill children, as well as children with special needs.

Disability Matters: Encouraging Every Church to Embrace Disability

WhyDisabilityMatters.org. Designed for churches, this website offers resources and coaching for those who want to develop ministries to embrace those within their congregations who have a disability.

Joni and Friends

JoniandFriends.org. This clearinghouse has resources for those with a disability, as well as for their friends and families, churches, and educators. Find a disability-friendly church near you, request prayer, and learn more about family retreats.

Not Alone: Finding Faith and Friendship for the Special-Needs Journey

SpecialNeedsParenting.net. Representing a wide variety of special needs, this community of bloggers offers faith and friendship through the journey.

Rising Above Ministries

RisingAboveMinistries.org. Based in Tennessee, this ministry offers national retreats, conferences, and workshops just for families like yours.

Snappin' Ministries

Snappin.org. Devoted to caring for caregivers, Snappin' offers retreats, mentoring opportunities, and an inspirational blog written by a large number of contributors.

ABOUT THE AUTHORS

K imberly M. Drew is a graduate of Taylor University with a degree in elementary education. She and her college sweetheart, Ryan, have been married since 2000 and live with their four children, Abigail, Jayden, Cooper, and Elizabeth. They also have a son, Jackson, who is waiting for them in heaven.

Kimberly developed a passion for children with special needs and their parents after their daughter Abigail suffered a traumatic birth that resulted in multiple disabilities, including cerebral palsy, a seizure disorder, hearing loss, and microcephaly. From these experiences, and from a heart to see and know Christ more, came the desire to help other parents grow in their Christian walk through their own experience raising a child with special needs. In 2016, she and Ryan adopted Elizabeth as an infant with special needs. In addition to her personal experience and her educational background, Kimberly has attended training sessions from Joni and Friends on meeting the spiritual needs of individuals with special needs and their families.

Since 2000, Kimberly has served as a pastor's wife and mentor to teenage girls. She and her family live in rural New Jersey, where Ryan is the youth pastor of his hometown church. Kimberly has led numerous

Bible studies over the years for teens and adults and is a public speaker at university classes and church groups. She is a regular contributor to DifferentDream.com. Visit her blog at PromisesandPerspective.blog spot.com.

Jocelyn Green is a multiple award–winning author of more than ten works of fiction and nonfiction, including the *Faith Deployed* and *Faith Deployed . . . Again* devotionals for military wives, *The Five Love Languages Military Edition* (with Dr. Gary Chapman), and the Heroines Behind the Lines Civil War series of novels.

Jocelyn's passion for special-needs families was ignited October 13, 2008, when her five-day-old son, Ethan, was diagnosed with congenital hypothyroidism, which causes dwarfism and profound mental disability. While daily medication has kept his development on track with his typical peers, Jocelyn's heart remains burdened for the special-needs child and parent.

Jocelyn graduated from Taylor University in Upland, Indiana, with a BA in English. She is also a public speaker and has addressed church groups, military gatherings, book clubs, civic groups, university classes, and writers' workshops. She is an active member of the Christian Authors Network, the Advanced Writers and Speakers Association, and American Christian Fiction Writers.

Jocelyn and her husband, Rob, have two children and live in Cedar Falls, Iowa. Visit her at JocelynGreen.com.

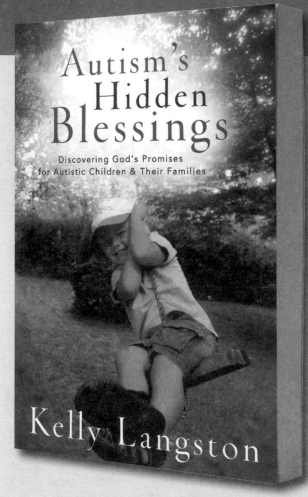